IMAGES of America

THE PINE BARRENS OF NEW JERSEY

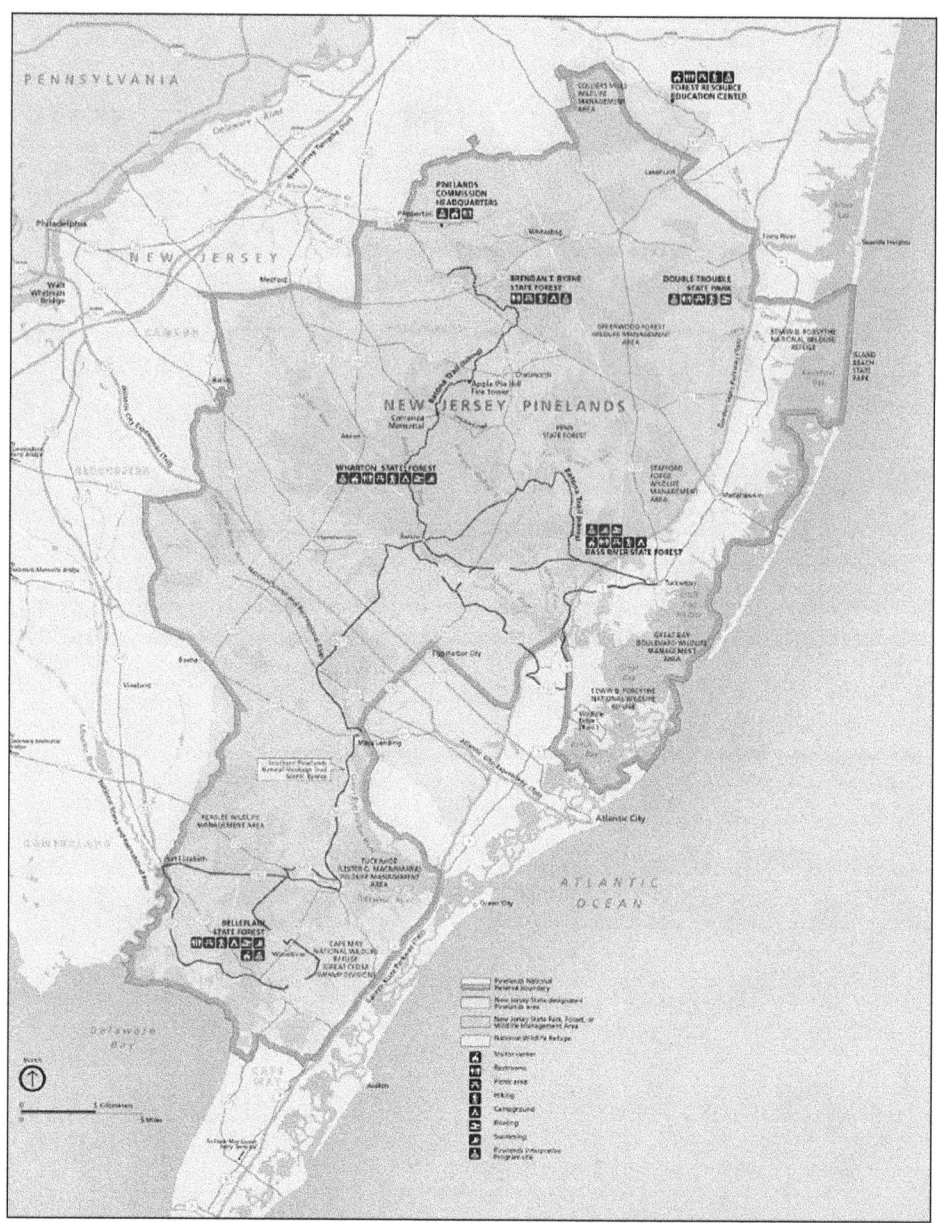

The Pine Barrens of New Jersey cover 22 percent of the state, encompassing parts of seven counties and 56 municipalities. The 1.1 million-acre Pinelands National Reserve is a federally protected area, established in 1978. New Jersey created the Pinelands area the following year, offering protection and preservation zones. While some land is privately held, there are several state parks and wildlife management areas within the region. (Courtesy of the Pinelands Commission.)

ON THE COVER: The cranberry is one of three indigenous fruits in the Pine Barrens; the other two are the blueberry and the grape. The flower of a cranberry resembles the head of a crane, and so they were first called "craneberries." Harvesting cranberries in the late 1800s and early 1900s was backbreaking, labor-intensive work. Harvesting was done by hand using a wooden or metal scoop. (Photograph by William F. Augustine; courtesy of Budd Wilson.)

IMAGES *of America*

THE PINE BARRENS OF NEW JERSEY

Karen F. Riley

ARCADIA
PUBLISHING

Copyright © 2010 by Karen F. Riley
ISBN 978-1-5316-4830-5

Published by Arcadia Publishing
Charleston, South Carolina

Library of Congress Control Number: 2010922154

For all general information contact Arcadia Publishing at:
Telephone 843-853-2070
Fax 843-853-0044
E-mail sales@arcadiapublishing.com
For customer service and orders:
Toll-Free 1-888-313-2665

Visit us on the Internet at www.arcadiapublishing.com

This book is dedicated to the people of the Pines and those who work to uncover and keep the history alive for generations to come.

CONTENTS

Foreword		6
Acknowledgments		8
Introduction		9
1.	Agriculture	11
2.	The Industries	23
3.	Labor and Seasonal Work	61
4.	People and Places	71
5.	Rails	87
6.	Proud to be a Piney	99
7.	Gone But Not Forgotten	111

FOREWORD

When I met John McPhee, I was in the field excavating the Batsto window-light factory. McPhee was collecting data for his articles, and then book, about the New Jersey Pine Barrens. McPhee wanted information about the iron industry. I said this was Pittsburgh. In *The Pine Barrens*, he calls the ironworks, once located there, "precursive Pittsburgh." McPhee profiled the culture of the people in the Pines and jump-started a process that, within a decade, led to both federal and state legislation to protect over a million acres. The natural beauty of the Pine Barrens is now known internationally. What remains less well-known is the story of the people and the towns and industry they created.

In 1978, the federal government created the Pinelands National Reserve. This was the first national reserve in the nation, and it combines both public and private lands. The next year, New Jersey created the Pinelands area. The state area is divided into a preservation zone and a protection zone. The federal area is larger but included tidal marsh. Each regulation affects more than 50 separate municipalities.

Over 1,000 prehistoric sites have been recorded in the Pine Barrens. A few of these sites are more than 10,000 years old and date from a time when the landscape was quite different. When the first European settlers arrived in the late 17th century, the Pine Barrens forest was well established.

The new settlers felled the large trees and made lumber. They took the medium-sized trees and made cordwood. Smaller timber (between 2 and 8 feet) was made into charcoal. Pitch pine was the predominant tree, but the white cedar was the most valuable. Since the 19th century, the pine forest has been cut at least five times. The last original white cedar forest was cut in the 1870s, and these stumps can measure over 4 feet in diameter.

Homes were built along the tidal rivers. Waterpowered sawmills were constructed above the head of navigational waters. Shipbuilding was an established industry by 1760. Two decades later, these ships were used by privateers to capture British vessels. By 1768, iron furnaces were producing cast iron and forges were hammering wrought iron, which became the major industry in the Pine Barrens. The furnace towns controlled the land where the charcoal was made and the bog ore was dug. The iron industry lasted almost 100 years. A glass industry flourished in the middle of the 19th century. There were also fulling mills, cotton mills, and paper mills. Then came the railroad. Whole new towns were created along the railroads, and the first tourists arrived. The common cranberry was turned into a major agricultural venture.

The first settlers were Swedes, Dutch, English, and Scottish immigrants who practiced subsistence agriculture. The ironworkers were English, Welsh, and Scotch-Irish. Furnace towns had gristmills and ground grain to feed both families and work animals. Later immigrants were German, Italian, and Russian, and these new groups were truck farmers with farms primarily outside the heart of the Pine Barrens. In the core area, cranberry-growing expanded rapidly and was later augmented by the blueberry cultivation.

A subculture developed among those people who worked the woods cutting cord wood and making charcoal; these people became known as "Pineys."

Part of the remnant subculture became the focus of an early 20th century study in eugenics. The study portrayed these people as feeble-minded, uneducated drunkards who had descended from a tavern wench nine generations before. The study called these people Pineys and suggested that they be sterilized.

The study proved to be a hoax, but not before it placed a stigma on all the people who worked the woods. There was no generational data. The photographic negatives were retouched and the people in the photographs were not from the Pine Barrens.

The term Piney grew to include not only people who worked the woods but also anyone living in the Pine Barrens over several generations and has even been applied to nonnative people who have come in to work the woods.

The plight of the Piney—from powerless to proud—is the cultural counterpart of the return of the bald eagle in the natural environment. Today, being a Piney is a badge worn proudly!

—Budd Wilson

Acknowledgments

A book of this magnitude cannot be written without the help and expertise of people in different fields. I am indebted to them for their kindness and time in helping me verify information and share with me their knowledge of the subjects about which they are passionate. They include Budd Wilson, Dennis Niceler, Tim Hart, Terry O'Leary, Rich Schaub, Joan Berkey, Dick Regensburg, Pete Stemmer, John Pearce, R. Marilyn Schmidt, Carol Reed, Mary Carty, Pola Galie, Maryann Kley, Dianne Wood, David Ashmen, Linda Stanton, Ted Gordon, Steve Eichinger, Cheryl Baisden, Jaclyn Stewart, Jeff Brower, Grove Conrad, Annie Brogan, Michael Hogan, Steve Maurer, Steve Lee III, Stephen Lee IV, Cathy Antener, Jim Keady, Candace Lillie, Bernard Graebener, June Sheridan, Eleanor Ditton, Mark Maxwell, Barbara Bolton, Judy Lipman, and Frank Ingram.

Thank you to all of the historical societies and organizations and their volunteers toiling to preserve memories of the past so they can educate the generations of the future, in particular Atlantic County Historical Society, New Jersey Forest Service, New Jersey Forest Fire Service, New Egypt Historical Society, Lacey Township Historical Society, Egg Harbor City Historical Society, Tuckerton Historical Society, Tuckerton Seaport, Burlington County Historical Society, Burlington County Library, Greate Egg Harbour Historical Society, Cumberland County Historical Society, Gloucester County Historical Society, Ocean County Cultural and Heritage Commission, Museum of American Glass, and Hagley Museum and Library.

Thank you to all of the Pine Barrens authors who have gone before me and inspired me, particularly John McPhee, Barbara Solem-Stull, Arthur Pierce, John Pearce, and George Flemming.

A special thank-you to my husband, Bill Riley, who patiently puts up with my long-night writing sessions and weekend jaunts in search of the next interview or cache of photographs. You have always supported my dreams, and I realize how blessed I am to have you in my life.

To Andrew Gioulis, my business partner and "creative eye" on this project, thank you for covering the office so I could work on this book and for your photographic expertise.

Thanks go to Erin Rocha, my editor, for believing in this project from the inception.

And most of all, thank you to the people of the Pine Barrens—for this is your history in the making. Without you, there would have been no story to tell.

INTRODUCTION

Budd Wilson has eloquently summed up the purpose and spirit of this book in his foreword. When I met him for the first time, he told me that he had planned to become a history teacher, but then the field of archaeology opened up at his college, and he switched to that. I humbly suggest that he has managed to do both successfully for many years, through the imparting of his wisdom and experience. Budd is just one of many incredible folks that I have been blessed to meet over the past 10 years since I started researching the Pine Barrens. Unlike Budd, I was not born here, and yet I have developed a passion and respect for this land and the people who live and work here.

The Pine Barrens occupies 22 percent of the most densely populated state in the country. Its 1.1 million acres are not "barren" at all, but teeming with life; almost 40 animal species on the state's threatened and endangered list reside here. There are plant species that exist here that are found nowhere else on earth, such as the bog asphodel. This striking member of the lily family blooms in late June, bursting forth with lacy yellow clusters of lily-like petaled flowers only four to nine millimeters in length. The bog asphodel once also existed in Delaware and the Carolinas but has been extirpated from those states. There are less than 3,000 remaining today.

I liken my experience in learning about the Pine Barrens to the bog asphodel. When we first moved here in 1992, I was a busy wife, mother, and employee in the corporate world. I loved living out in the country, since I had grown up in the city and wanted to raise my children in a rural environment. But other than beauty and quiet, quite frankly, the edge of the Pine Barrens outside my door was . . . well, a nice stand of trees.

I say this because you may be thinking the same thing. You may or may not have ever heard of the Pine Barrens before picking up this book. You may live here and know little about this area, or you may be a Pine Barrens enthusiast looking to increase your knowledge. Whatever your vantage point, I suggest you consider the bog asphodel. It is out there, whether you know of its existence or not. Because of its size, you may go in search of it and never find it. Perhaps you have never been told of its wonders and, like I am, remain caught up in this frenzied world.

The intention of this book is to take you out of that world—even for a brief time—and take you deep into the woods to help you learn about the charcoal burners who stayed in the forest day and night for two weeks at a time to make a product that you may toss on your barbecue grill without a thought, to discover ghost towns and villages whose names only exist on old maps, and to learn about the special and unique people who were born on this soil and whose labor and love made a difference in this land. There are those who made history: John Mason and his patented jar; Elizabeth Lee, creator of canned cranberry sauce; and Elizabeth White, who helped cultivate blueberries. There are also little known people and inventions that have made a difference. There are forest firefighters whom you may never have met but whom you might owe your life or your dwelling to. There are archaeologists like Budd Wilson, unraveling the mysteries of the past so we can learn more about the bog iron industries, the glass factories, and the paper mills. There are dozens of writers, like George Flemming, who spent 50 years doing research that culminated in the publication of *Brotherton*, which helped us learn about the people who worked this land first, before the settlers arrived.

It is not possible to truly expose you to the wealth and riches of the Pine Barrens in a book this size. You could read an entire section of books from the Pine Barrens genre (yes, it has its own genre!) and still be left wanting. You may finish this book and disagree with choices I made and what I included. You may be wondering why I have covered some things and left out others. It was a very difficult choice to make, but ultimately, my purpose in bringing you this book is simply to whet your appetite, to let you know that there is a bog asphodel waiting in the woods for you. When you have finished reading, I hope you are filled with awe for the incredible place that the Pine Barrens is. I know it still continues to take my breath away, and I hope you come to feel the same way.

If you have learned something from this book when you are done, then I hope to encourage you to discover more. There is a wealth of knowledge waiting at your fingertips, through other books, the volunteers at the many historical societies throughout the area, and, most of all, the people who have chosen to make the Pine Barrens their home. Seek them out, ask them questions, and listen to the passion in their voices as they share their treasures. October is Pine Barrens month. Each year, educators, organizations, and private individuals come together to impart their knowledge and share their world with you. Visit one of the free events, listen to the beautiful music of the Pines, breathe in deeply that wonderful earthy smell, and be prepared to have your heart changed forever.

The Pine Barrens is not just a place. It is not just a culture. It is a way of life that, sadly, we lose more of each day. The old-fashioned way of doing things is giving way more and more to modern technology. In some ways, this is progress, such as cranberry growers seeing larger yields each year on the same acreage or, in some cases, even less land. But areas that are not preserved are being trampled under bulldozers as another housing development sprouts up. Older Pineys are dying off, and their children may now live in other states. We all have choices to make. Modern medicine, technology, and industry have made incredible advances. But out there in the woods, there is still a tiny yellow flower that probably looks the same as its ancestors hundreds of years ago. It is just waiting for you to discover it.

One

AGRICULTURE

Elizabeth Coleman White, the daughter of cranberry farmers, worked from 1911 to 1916 with Dr. Frederick V. Coville, a botanist from the U.S. Department of Agriculture, to develop and cultivate a marketable blueberry in Whitesbog. Highbush blueberries grow wild in the Pine Barrens, and Elizabeth drew on locals' knowledge to find bushes that she could use in her experiments. (Photograph by William F. Augustine; courtesy of Budd Wilson.)

Cranberry labels, such as the one above, were used by growers to establish their brands, with the objective being to demonstrate a level of quality that would become associated with that name. Labels also depicted the time of harvest. The Sunrise brand was available after the 20th of October. (Courtesy of R. Marilyn Schmidt.)

In the 19th and the first part of the 20th centuries, cranberries were picked by hand. It was a backbreaking job to tediously remove all of the berries from the vines. Many were missed, and the process was time consuming and vines could be badly damaged, but no other means existed yet. Children as young as three would help other family members in the bogs. Millie Cornaro (right), age 10, began picking at age four. (Courtesy of the Library of Congress.)

Entire families would participate in the cranberry harvest. Children missed several weeks of school during September and October to help their families earn money. Both of these families are from Pennsylvania and will live in shacks next to the bogs until the season is over and then return home. Richard Trevor (above foreground), age eight, has been picking berries each of the five previous seasons. Jennie Camillo (right), also eight, carries a 15-pound box of cranberries to the checking station. (Both, courtesy of the Library of Congress.)

A young boy is headed back out to the bog after dropping off cranberries at the checking station. Pickers were responsible for completely filling their containers with clean, undamaged berries. If the collection were satisfactory, the inspector would give the picker a ticket that he could redeem later for goods or cash. (Photograph by Arthur Rothstein; courtesy of the Library of Congress.)

Families would live in small shacks, like this one near Pemberton, during the picking season, which could last six to eight weeks. All 10 of the DeMarco family members stayed in this 10- by 11-foot shack. (Courtesy of the Library of Congress.)

Women are sorting cranberries by hand around 1880 in this photograph taken at Double Trouble (above). This was a very tedious job each autumn as they hand checked for damaged fruit and removed leaves and vine material from cranberries piled in the bins. Conveyor belts (below) would make selecting the fruit only slightly easier. In its sorting and packinghouse, Double Trouble had an Otis elevator. Berries would be transported to the top of the building via the elevator and then released. Good berries will bounce; bad ones will not. Today the entire process is automated. (Both, courtesy of Ocean County Cultural and Heritage Commission.)

Cranberry packinghouses, like the one in Vincentown pictured above, were used for the sorting of fresh fruit. Cranberries can be harvested by either a dry or a wet method. The dry method is used for fresh cranberries, while the wet is for berries used in juice, sauce, and items like Craisins. The wet method involves flooding the bog when it is time to harvest; since cranberries contain air chambers, they will float. The vines are trained to grow in certain directions to minimize damage from the machines (below). The man walking in front with a stick is checking the direction of the vines. The harvesting machine, with its gently swirling reels, will knock the berries off the vine so they can be easily collected. This photograph was taken in the Chatsworth area. (Above, courtesy of the Burlington County Library; below, courtesy of photographer Andrew Gioulis.)

Floating berries are corralled by flexible material called a cran-boom (above). A machine set up in the center of the enclosed area will pump the berries and water up to the cranberry cleaner seen in the background. The berries are spray-washed (below), and leaves and vine materials will fall through the screen seen at the right. These will be composted. Nothing goes to waste during a cranberry harvest. The water in the cleaner and in the flooded bog will be used for the next bog, and so on until the end of harvest, when it is returned to the river. The truck seen on the left will bring the berries to the Ocean Spray Receiving Station located nearby. Each truck holds 300 barrels of cranberries, equivalent to 30,000 pounds of fruit. (Both, courtesy of photographer Andrew Gioulis.)

Grapes are one of three indigenous fruits in this area; blueberries and cranberries are the other two. Renault "monuments," like the one shown above, dot the landscape of Egg Harbor City to promote the town's famous company. Founded in 1864, Renault is the oldest continuous commercial winemaker in New Jersey. Even during Prohibition, Renault stayed in business by producing sacramental wines and Renault Wine Tonic, a 22 percent alcohol brew sold in pharmacies for a variety of ailments. On the other end of the grape spectrum is Dr. Thomas Welch (left), a Vineland dentist who used grapes from local vineyards and pasteurized them to make the world's first "unfermented wine," today known as grape juice. (Above, courtesy of the Egg Harbor City Historical Society; left, courtesy of the Vineland Historical Society.)

Welch first bottled his product in 1869 to use at his church's communion service. Sales of ceremonial quality grape juice to other churches throughout southern New Jersey and southeastern Pennsylvania soon followed. The Welch's Grape Juice Factory in Vineland (pictured above and below) was having trouble keeping up with the demand because quality grapes were in short supply. Vineyards in the Vineland area were susceptible to grape rot disease. Dr. Welsh and his son, Dr. Charles Welsh, decided to move the business to New York State in 1896. (Both, courtesy of the Vineland Historical Society.)

The Vineland Grape Juice Company was formed by a group of investors who were disappointed that Welch relocated his plant. The Vineland company used some of the equipment left behind by Welch. The factory thrived until a fire destroyed the building in 1913. It was never rebuilt. (Courtesy of the Vineland Historical Society.)

Tomatoes are another crop that thrives in acidic soil. Back in the Middle Ages, many people believed tomatoes were poisonous and called them the Devil's Fruit. This is a tomato-canning factory in New Egypt, built near the railroad station. The boy on the steps is Thomas Van Horn. (Courtesy of the New Egypt Historical Society.)

Settlers to the Pine Barrens quickly learned that the sandy, acidic soil was not conducive to most crops and turned in time to cultivating cranberries and blueberries. However, the outer lying areas like Cumberland County in the southwest corner and New Egypt, in the northern section of the Pine Barrens had more fertile, loamy soil that allowed for other varieties of crops to thrive. (Courtesy of the Cumberland County Historical Society.)

Oxen were often used in farming. Owned by John Leary of Vincentown, this harnessed team was one of the last known to be used in Burlington County. This photograph was taken on the Leary farm in June 1908. In a cart hitched to his goat, the future farmer-in-training rides alongside the larger wagon. (Photograph by Nathaniel R. Ewan; courtesy of the Burlington County Library.)

John L. Mason (left) of New York City invented and patented the now famous Mason jar (below) on November 30, 1858. He designed the jar to be air- and watertight. The manufacturing process stated on his patent application called for the glass jar to be made in a mold as opposed to the spinning method, allowing better control of the screw thread design. The other main components of the form were to have the screw thread extend to the top of the jar to ensure an airtight seal. The threading would not go all the way to the edge, but meet with a groove. Once the patent was approved, Mason set up a plant in Vineland where he manufactured the jars. (Both, courtesy of the Vineland Historical Society.)

Two
THE INDUSTRIES

In 1806, James Lee and others built the first glass factory in Millville. This area along the banks of the Maurice River became known as Glasstown. The factory was renamed Whitall Tatum and Company in 1848. By 1876, the facility was making a variety of medicine, apothecary, show, perfume, and poison bottles, food storage containers, and carboys in a wide range of colors. (Courtesy of the Museum of American Glass, Millville.)

Emil Larson (left) was a decorative glassblower who worked for the Durand Art Glass division of the Vineland Flint Glass Works from 1924 to 1931. He opened his own backyard shop in Vineland after Durand closed. Ralph Barber (below) worked at the Whitall Tatum Company, where the glassblowers were allowed to make glass for themselves on their own time. Barber is legendary for his Millville Rose paperweights. In 1912, Barber left Millville to become superintendent of the Vineland Flint Glass Works owned by Victor Durand. Barber supervised the skilled department that produced x-ray tubes. It was while in charge of this department that the American Institute of Glass named Barber "the greatest glassblower in the United States." (Both, courtesy of the Museum of American Glass, Millville.)

The Great Depression had a significant impact on glassmaking in New Jersey, as factories closed and workers faced unemployment. The United States government formed the Works Progress Administration (WPA) to put people to work nationwide. The WPA set up a glass factory in Vineland that was managed by Frank Dougherty Sr. WPA workers are shown here performing paste mold blowing. Thin cast iron molds were used with a carbon paste on the surface. As the wet mold contacted the hot glass, the steam vapor allowed the piece to be twirled as the worker blew into the pipe, eliminating the mold line. (Both, photographs by Lewis K. Hine; courtesy of the Museum of American Glass, Millville.)

Theodore Corson Wheaton was born in Tuckahoe, New Jersey, in 1852. He graduated from the Medical College of Pennsylvania in 1879 and established himself as a country doctor. Between 1883 and 1892, while living in Millville, Dr. Wheaton operated three drugstores and a general store in conjunction with his medical practice. It is not surprising that this energetic doctor became interested in pharmacists' and physicians' glassware. In 1888, Dr. Wheaton became involved in the financing of a Millville glass factory. By 1890, he was the sole owner and the company was renamed the T. C. Wheaton Company. (Courtesy of the Museum of American Glass, Millville.)

Women also worked in the factory at the T. C. Wheaton Company. In the c. 1890 photograph above, workers are tying stoppers to bottles. Below, employees pose on the Old Spice assembly line around 1942. Old Spice bottles were originally made of pottery by the A. E. Hull Pottery Company in Crooksville, Ohio. The first glass bottles were manufactured by Wheaton after several months spent developing the right blend of materials to give the new bottles a "pottery appearance." (Both, courtesy of the Museum of American Glass, Millville.)

At age 80, Charles Pepper is hard at work making a carboy—a large glass bottle used to hold liquids—at Wheaton Glass Company around 1948. He was born in 1868 just outside of Millville and began working at Whitall Tatum in Millville as a "tending boy" when he was nine years old. (Courtesy of the Museum of American Glass, Millville.)

The two blowpipe mouthpieces pictured here are called bebees. The one on the left was excavated at Batsto Window Glass Factory between 1965 and 1967. The one on the right belonged to Bill Breeden of Burlington. (Courtesy of Budd Wilson.)

Charles Read built Batsto Ironworks by the mouth of Batsto River in 1766. In 1784, it was taken over by William Richards and then managed by his son, Jesse, after William retired in 1809. Batsto continued to prosper until the middle of the 19th century, when sources of bog iron became depleted and Pennsylvania's ironworks began producing a purer grade of iron ore with anthracite coal, a better smelting agent than charcoal. Jesse Richards and James M. Brookfield went into partnership in 1845 to manufacture glass at New Columbia, now called Nesco, several miles west of Batsto. In May 1846, Jesse opened a second glassworks, this time at Batsto. It manufactured flat glass for windows using the cylinder method. Panes of glass were called lights. Glass was turned and shaped in "swing pits" shown above. (Both, courtesy of Budd Wilson.)

When William Richards died in 1823, the estate was sold to Thomas Richards, a grandnephew. Jesse later secured ownership with a $13,425 mortgage on the property. When he died in 1854, his eldest son, also named Thomas, took it over. Mortgage debt, economic crises, and frequent repairs took a toll, and Batsto was sold in 1876 for $14,000 to Joseph Wharton. The Wharton family is shown below in front of the Batsto mansion around 1880. They are, from left to right, Anna, Joseph, Mrs. Wharton (partially hidden behind Joseph), Mary, and Joanna (on horse). The attendant is unidentified. (Above, courtesy of Budd Wilson; below, courtesy of Ruth Gerber.)

Above is the melting furnace at Estellville Glass Factory. The Pine Barrens was full of sand used to make glass, but minute amounts of iron in the sand made it difficult to manufacture clear glass. The sand was mixed with lime and potash and melted into glass. A glassblower had to be a master craftsman, able to handle 100 pounds of blowpipe and molten glass and, within five to 10 minutes, turn it into a cylinder 10 inches wide, five feet long, and an eighth-inch thick. Some blowers would chain themselves to a post to counterbalance the weight. They were paid not for what they blew, but for how many boxes of usable glass they could produce. Fires were a frequent occurrence at furnaces, as seen below at Estellville. (Above, courtesy of photographer Andrew Gioulis; below, courtesy of Budd Wilson.)

Nicholas Sooy II owned thousands of acres along the Mullica River and lived in this house. It was built in three sections, the first reflecting the Revolutionary period to which it dates and the second and third sections believed to have been added by his nephew, Nicholas Sooy III. (Courtesy of Budd Wilson.)

In 1869, John H. Rapp and Francis Wing leased part of the land next to the Sooy homestead to start a glass factory. They hired Joseph Wapler to build the factory and several workers's homes, giving the village the name of Herman (sometimes spelled Hermann or Hermon) City. The factory primarily made clear glass. It only lasted six months and few ruins remain. (Courtesy of the New Jersey Forest Service.)

Glassmaking was actually one of the last industries in the Pines, and glass is still made today in areas like Millville and Vineland. One of the first industries in the Pine Barrens was charcoal making. Charcoal use in the process of glassmaking dates back to Egyptian times, and it is often made in connection with mining and smelting. A successful bog iron furnace used at least 20,000 acres of timber. It took almost four cords of wood to make 100 bushels of charcoal. After the cords were cut, a pole called a fergen (sometimes fergin or fagan) was placed in the center of the field (left) with cords of wood stacked around it in a teepee fashion (below). (Both, courtesy of the New Jersey Forest Service.)

Layers of turf called floats were then packed onto the sides of the pit to prevent air from escaping. The person tending the pit was called a collier. Early colliers, of course, did not have the advantage of trucking their turf to the site, as seen here. (Courtesy of the New Jersey Forest Service.)

Turf was applied with rakes, and because the pit was usually taller than the collier, a rudimentary ladder was sometimes fashioned. The ladder was also used so the collier could check on the fire's intensity during the two weeks it would take for the charcoal process to finish. (Courtesy of the New Jersey Forest Service.)

The charcoal pit was blackened by covering the turf with a four-to-six-inch layer of sand. The fergen was pulled out and kindling dropped in to start a fire. Once it was started, more wood would be added and the top covered. The sharpened fergen would be used to punch draft holes in the bottom (above). A collier would watch the color of the smoke. Blue smoke meant the fire was too hot, so he would plug some holes with sand. If the fire became too hot, the wood would burn instead of char. The color of the smoke would also let the collier know when the process was complete. (Both, courtesy of the New Jersey Forest Service.)

An experienced collier could watch up to 20 pits at a time. Colliers stayed in the woods through the entire process, sleeping alongside the pits so they could closely watch the fires. They often kept a dog with them (above). When the charcoal was done, the collier poured sand into the opening to extinguish the flames and push out any remaining air. Charcoal was highly combustible and exposing it to air could cause the entire pit to explode. Coals were gradually cooled and packed in 30-35 pound bags (below). Mules would pull specially designed boxes that allowed the coal to be dumped out easily. Coal that was not used locally was often transported to New York and Philadelphia. The last documented pit in Ocean County was extinguished in 1976. (Both, courtesy of the New Jersey Forest Service.)

Sawmills quickly sprang up throughout the Pines, harnessing the waterpower to turn oak, pine, and cedar into lumber for houses and ships. The forests were decimated so quickly that in 1749, Benjamin Franklin spoke of the "reckless and wanton slaughter of the woods." He urged that appropriate forestry practices and conservation be instituted. Each iron furnace required 30 square miles of timber, which was clear-cut on a 20-year cycle. In the photograph above, 10 cords of wood are being moved through Vanhiseville, in Ocean County, in January 1926. (Both, courtesy of the New Jersey Forest Service.)

Signs in this woodworker's shop reflect the hard times experienced by many in the Pine Barrens. One reads, "Since man has been so unjust I hardly know what man to trust. I trusted many to my sorrow so pay today and I trust tomorrow." The other sign states, "Please don't ask for trust. Old trust is dead. Poor pay killed him." (Courtesy of the New Jersey Forest Service.)

A 1713 act was passed in the colony of New Jersey for protection of pine and cedar timber. But large shipments of oak, white cedar, sassafras, and pine were transported to New York and Philadelphia from 1840 to 1880. Pitch pine was cut to produce charcoal, turpentine, axle grease, and torches. This sawmill is at New Lisbon. (Courtesy of the Burlington County Historical Society.)

In the early 1900s, there were 18 basket-manufacturing companies in Plumsted alone. White or post oak was traditionally used, although other materials were sometimes incorporated. Many basketmakers used a shave horse (below), which they normally built themselves. Some of those basketmakers are shown here with their work (above). (Above, courtesy of the New Egypt Historical Society; below, courtesy of the New Jersey Forest Service.)

A worker is cutting veneer cores into bolts (above), which will be used for basket bottoms. Below, the tops of baskets are being nailed on. These c. 1945 photographs were taken at the Vineland location of the New Jersey Package Plant. The wood being used is likely yellow poplar, as Vineland supported a good growth of these trees. Baskets were also made out of white or post oak. Members of the red oak family were typically used for making pallets and for flooring. (Both, courtesy of the New Jersey Forest Service.)

Shipbuilding was a huge industry from around 1760 to 1860. White oak, white pine, and cedar were the chief woods used. Boatworks were located at the headwaters of most coastal streams. Huge timbers would be hewn into schooners, sloops, and catboats. These photographs were taken in Cape May around 1880. Smuggling was also a widespread occupation until it was outlawed in 1774. Privateering, which was basically the same activity, was legalized at the beginning of the American Revolution. It was easier and more profitable to board a ship and take goods than sail to New York or Philadelphia to procure them. (Both, courtesy of the New Jersey Forest Service.)

Joe Ware (left) and Ed Weber are cutting shingles in Lower Bank (above). Ware bought some used sawmill machinery that he could move around, originally in Sandy Ridge, then New Gretna, and then Lower Bank. The mill had a 20-horsepower Fairbanks Morse kerosene engine, along with a log carriage, rip saw, and a shingle machine. Wood shingles were typically made of white pine or North Atlantic white cedar. Barrels, such as the ones being made at Elwood Potter's cottage on Park Avenue (below) around 1900, used white cedar or oak. Whiskey barrels would be singed to seal. Cranberry barrels would be left with openings between the slats so the fruit could breathe. (Above, courtesy of Pete Stemmer; below, courtesy of the Vineland Historical Society.)

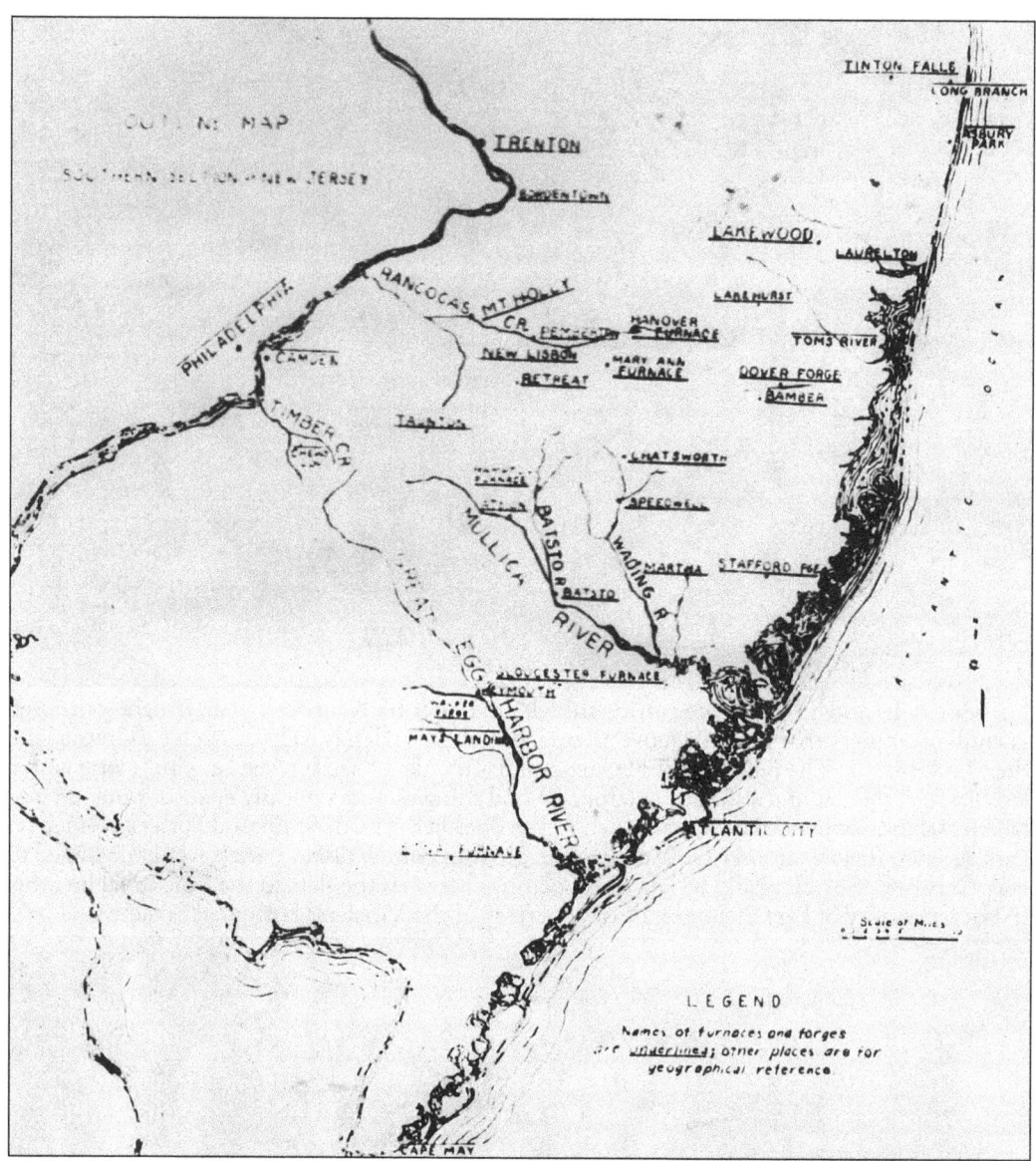

The first record of bog iron mining in New Jersey was the Tinton Falls Iron Works, established in 1675. Bog iron is formed by a complex chemical process that takes place between decaying vegetation that builds up in the rivers and beds and the iron salts found there. In many areas of the Pine Barrens, the bottom of the streambed is made up of marl, or greensand, which contains iron. The iron oxidizes as it is carried to the surface of the water and then becomes deposited along the banks, where it mixes with mud and hardens into rocky ore beds. Bog iron is then mined from the swamps and transported to the furnaces for smelting. At least 17 furnaces and forges were built in the Pine Barrens. (Courtesy of the New Jersey Forest Service.)

Besides bog iron, the Pine Barrens contained two other key ingredients for smelting: waterpower and fuel. Streams powered the bellows to keep the furnace going. Put into blast in the spring when the water wheel thawed, furnaces ran 24 hours a day until December or January, when it froze. Charcoal provided the fuel. As the streambeds were mined, ore was gathered in ore boats and brought ashore. This boat is being excavated from the Batsto River, using barrels as floats. (Photograph by Burrel Adams; courtesy of Pete Stemmer.)

James Starkey (left), archaeologist, and Batsto Citizens Committee charter members Howard R. Kemble (center) and John D. F. Morgan examine the boat more closely. (Courtesy of Gloucester County Historical Society.)

In the Revolutionary War, Batsto provided the Continental army with iron fittings, cannons, cannonballs, and pans for desalinating saltwater. Workers were exempt from military service because of the importance of products made. They also produced stoves, firebacks, nails, kettles, and water pipes. George Washington purchased four monogrammed Batsto firebacks in the 1780s; two remain at Mount Vernon. (Both, courtesy of Gloucester County Historical Society.)

Batsto workers rented cottages like these for $2 a month in 1878. Village rules for workers included completing chores before 6:00 a.m., at which time work would begin, and no unnecessary talking or noise during work. Another rule was: "Doors and gates must be kept habitually shut. If necessarily opened, must be fastened and in no case allowed to swing in the wind." It was also noted that "laziness and slovenly habits will not be tolerated." Some of the workers are shown below on Main Street. (Above, courtesy of the Library of Congress; below, courtesy of Budd Wilson.)

After several owners, the town that became Harrisville was sold to William McCarty, Thomas Davis, and Isaac Ashmead for $7,000 by Samuel Richards, owner of Atsion, part-owner of Martha and Speedwell furnaces, and brother of Jesse, Batsto's owner. It was promptly named McCartyville. McCarty decided to erect a paper mill at the site, though there were already at least 29 other paper mills in the state in 1834. He also built a new dam, a gristmill, a sawmill, a company store, and housing. Richard Harris, a former employee, eventually purchased the property in 1856. He and his father, John Harris, became the owners of Harrisville. (Both, courtesy of Pete Stemmer.)

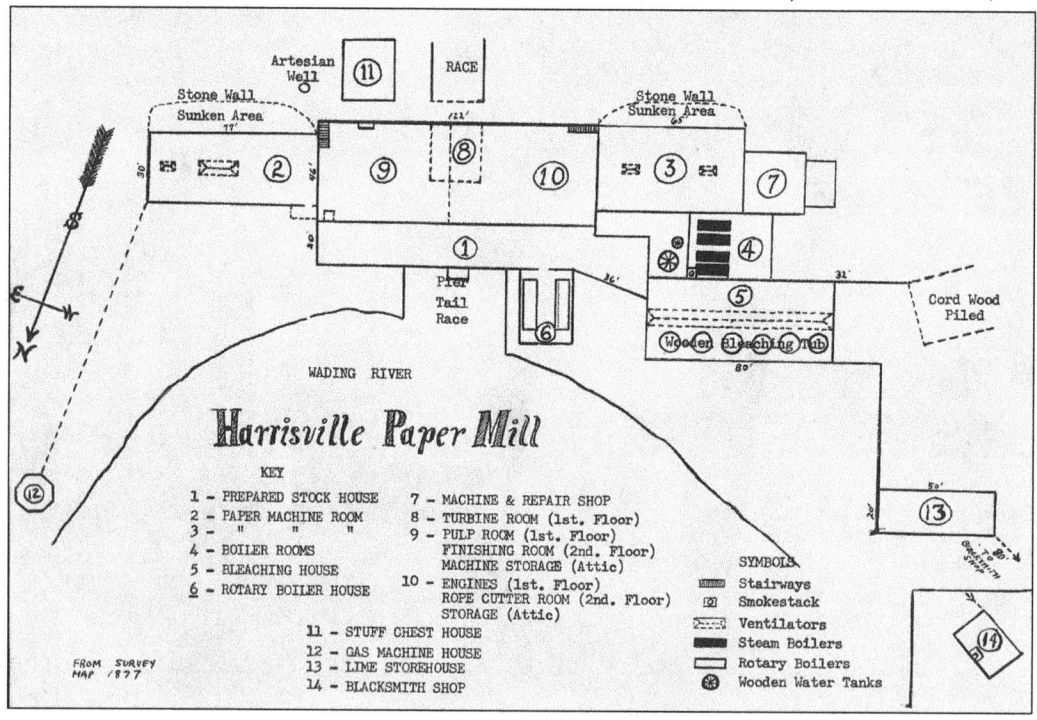

The Harrisville Manufacturing Company incorporated in 1865. The mill used salt hay from the Mullica River as a paper source. It was brought to the landing by barges and then delivered by mule teams (below). The salt hay was bought for $3 a ton. The iron content of the water gave the paper a strange brown color, like butcher's paper, and all attempts to make it white failed. Despite this, the mill prospered until the Harris family defaulted on a mortgage in 1890. The photograph below shows the north end of the main plant at Harrisville. One of the mansions is seen in the background at the upper right. This photograph was taken from a tintype, possibly from the late 1850s or early 1860s. (Above, photograph by Howard Feyl, courtesy of Budd Wilson; below, courtesy of Steve Eichinger.)

Harrisville was eventually purchased by Joseph Wharton in 1896, although the mill was no longer operating at that time. The gristmill is on the right (above). On the left is the company store. The paper mill cannot be seen here, but it was behind and to the right of the gristmill. Next to the store was the Broome Mansion (not seen here), where the last manager, Mahlon Broome, lived, and beyond that was the Harris Mansion. A 1914 fire devastated the town (below). (Both, photographs by Howard Feyl; courtesy of Budd Wilson.)

Dr. M. S. Lyon, president of the local YMCA, approached Wharton about using Harrisville for a summer boys' camp, but Wharton refused. Wharton died in 1909 and Lyon got permission from the estate to start Camp Lyon the following year. Howard Feyl attended the camp as a teen. (Photograph by Howard Feyl; courtesy of Budd Wilson.)

Little remains of Harrisville today and what does is protected by a high fence. The tallest remaining wall was once the west wall of the central portion of the main mill, measuring 122 feet long and three stories high. The raceway passed through the center of the mill, powering the turbines and then flowing out through the brick archways seen here. (Courtesy of the New Jersey Forest Service.)

The subjects of these two photographs have been the center of much debate. The image above has been identified as either Harrisville or Weymouth. Evidence was raised in *Heart of the Pines* that seems to indicate it is indeed Harrisville and is commonly shown in reverse. The photograph below is either Speedwell or Hanover Furnace, the latter located near Whitesbog. There is a common wildflower named speedwell that the town is believed to have been named for. The town was the site of both a sawmill and an iron furnace that was located too far from navigable water and was never profitable. Hanover furnace was built in 1791 to 1792 by Ridgeway, Howell, Lacey, and Earl and closed around 1863 to 1864. (Above, courtesy of the Greate Egg Harbour Historical Society; below, courtesy of the Burlington County Historical Society.)

Benjamin Randolph was a cabinetmaker from Philadelphia. He lived in this house from 1785 until his death. He owned and operated Speedwell Furnace but is better known as the maker of a set of chairs that fetched a price of $33,000. He also made the desk on which Thomas Jefferson signed the Declaration of Independence. (Courtesy of the Burlington County Historical Society.)

The ruins of the town of Friendship lie at the end of Friendship-Speedwell Road. Speedwell Furnace once stood at the head of that road. In 1869, Friendship was a thriving cranberry village with a school, store, cranberry sorting and packinghouse, a manager's house, foremen's homes, and smaller dwellings for seasonal pickers. (Courtesy of photographer Andrew Gioulis.)

Philadelphia iron baron Isaac Potts built Martha Furnace in 1793, naming it after his wife. Two years later, he erected Wading River Forge and Slitting Mill 1.5 miles south of Martha, in a town later known as Harrisville. Ore, flux, and charcoal were heated until the iron separated and collected; it was channeled into troughs called pigs, hence the name pig iron. Forges further refined the process. Pig iron from Martha was brought to the slitting mill and made into nails. Martha Furnace's ruins were excavated by Budd Wilson in the 1960s. (Both, courtesy of Budd Wilson.)

The Honorable Charles Read held many political titles, including member of the assembly, judge of the Supreme Court, and chief justice of the Supreme Court of New Jersey. He was also a man of vision and saw himself prospering from the "black gold" of the Pine Barrens, bog iron. He erected Batsto Furnace and Atsion Forge within a year of each other. But he overextended himself financially and died destitute in 1774. Atsion became prosperous under new ownership from the bog iron Read dreamed of. Samuel Richards took full ownership in 1824, rebuilding the forge and adding a mansion, a company store, and a church to the property. Atsion went through more changes after Richard's death, including the addition of a cotton mill (above). (Both, courtesy of the Burlington County Library.)

The Colwell Mansion (above) was described in newspapers as "the finest in South Jersey." Built by Stephen Colwell in the mid-1800s, the home had an observatory, "an interesting wheel shaped round window with 12 spokes in it," long French windows, and hardwood fireplaces. The Colwell family acquired the Weymouth property in 1865. In 1808, Samuel Richards and Joseph Ball bought a controlling interest in the Weymouth Furnace Company. Richards's daughter, Sarah, married Stephen Colwell in 1836, and he became active in managing the operation. These ruins (below) are believed to be the Samuel Richards Mansion, later known as the Manager's House. (Above, courtesy of Budd Wilson; below, courtesy of the Burlington County Library.)

The first paper mill to be erected on the Weymouth property was the Atlantic Paper Mill. The site is now part of the Atlantic County Park System, and the 60-foot smokestack and arches over the millrace are still visible. It is believed to have been built over either the old furnace or forge site. The Weymouth Paper Mill was the second mill to be built here, and its millrace is also visible. The photograph below shows the remains of the pulp mixing vats. (Above, courtesy of photographer Andrew Gioulis; below, courtesy of the Atlantic County Historical Society.)

In 1822, Benjamin Richards erected a 3,000-spindle cotton mill on the site of a former sawmill. Pleasant Mills operated until 1855, when it was destroyed by fire. It began a life as a paper mill in 1861, when it was purchased by Thomas Irving and John McNeil. Fire struck again in 1878. A new paper mill was built on the site in 1880, which operated as Pleasant Mills Paper Company until 1915. It closed its doors in 1925. During its operation, the mill made kraft paper, document paper for the federal government, and sandpaper stock. These were made from manila rope, jute, and salt hay from the banks of the Mullica River. (Both, courtesy of the Atlantic County Historical Society.)

The Brooksbrae Brick Company was built in 1905. It is also referred to as the Pasadena Terra Cotta Company by Henry Charlton Beck in *Forgotten Towns of Southern New Jersey*. It is believed that the owner died before operations could commence. These photographs show the remains of the drying tunnels. A current of hot air would have been forced through the openings shown at right by a downdraft furnace. This would remove the moisture from the clay bricks before baking them in a downdraft kiln. (Both, courtesy of photographer Andrew Gioulis.)

Farmers would bring corn and grain to the local gristmill to be ground into flour or meal. The Williams Grist Mill in Pemberton relied on waterpower from the Jones Run branch of Indian Run. Williams, in the foreground, owned eight acres of land in addition to the gristmill when this photograph was taken in May 1894. (Photograph by Nathaniel R. Ewan; courtesy of the Burlington County Historical Society.)

Aetna (or Etna) Furnace was erected in Tuckahoe in 1816 by John Coates and the Howell family of Philadelphia. At its peak, 200 men worked here. Besides the furnace, there was a sawmill, gristmill, and 50 homes. The furnace ceased operations in 1832. This photograph was taken February 23, 1898. (Photograph by L. G. Reeve; courtesy of Steve Eichinger.)

Three

LABOR AND SEASONAL WORK

Many in the Pine Barrens followed the seasons for a means of income. In the summer months, there were blueberries to pick; fall ushered in the cranberry harvest. Mossing could be done any time the swamps were not frozen. Pinecones were picked for sale to florists. Age was no barrier, as everyone brought in money for the family in whatever way he or she could. (Photograph by William F. Augustine; courtesy of Pete Stemmer.)

"Pineballing" was the Piney name given to collecting pinecones for sale to florists, usually in New York City or Philadelphia. This activity was typically done in the Pygmy Pines area since the short tree size made the cones more accessible. Cones were usually collected after the first frost when there was less pitch in the stem and they could be snapped off the tree more easily. (Courtesy of the New Jersey Forest Service.)

The cones that Sam Ford from Herman City has in his basket have already opened. Pinecones remain closed until they are exposed to a high heat source like a forest fire, which softens the resin coating and allows the cone to open up. Many pick green cones that need to be heated up in makeshift "pinecone poppers" before being sold. (Photograph by William F. Augustine, courtesy of Pete Stemmer.)

"Mossing" was another common activity in the Pine Barrens. Sphagnum moss is a unique plant. It is able to absorb moisture up to five times its own weight. The secret lies in its intricate matrix of capillaries and surrounding air spaces, allowing water to be trapped and held like a sponge. Because of its absorption properties, Native Americans used the moss for diapers, and it was used during wartime for bandages. Today, florists use it to support floral arrangements and keep them moist. Mainly due to the weight of the waterlogged plant, pulling moss from the bogs with a moss rake is tough, hard work for men like Sam Ford (right). Once it is collected, it is spread out in open fields to dry and put into a moss press like the one Ford is using (below) to further squeeze out the moisture and compress them into bales. (Both, photographs by William F. Augustine; courtesy of Pete Stemmer.)

Born to German immigrants, Charlie Weber (left) was one of the last salt hayers in South Jersey. He rented salt hay meadows on the lower Wading River and harvested them each year. Salt hay was used as packing material for glassware, in the pit-casting process for manufacturing iron pipe, and in road construction. Paper mills, like Harrisville, experimented with using salt hay. Weber would take his horses, Prince and Kate, and walk over 20 miles harvesting the hay. It was loaded onto a barge on the Mullica River and taken upstream to dry land for baling and shipment. Covering protects the horses (below) from mosquitoes and greenhead flies. (Both, photographs by William F. Augustine; courtesy of Pete Stemmer.)

Every December for a week, men would fill hunting clubs scattered throughout the Pines for deer hunting season. In front of the American House Hunt Club in 1953 (above), are, from left to right, (kneeling) Woody Reynolds, Old Don Crammer, and Jim Garafalo; (standing) Robert Southard, unidentified, Jew Archer, Walter Miller, Charles Pullen, Young Don Crammer, Pete Reynolds, Joe Malloy, Stead Bishop, unidentified, Doc Wharton, John Inman, Frankie Green, and Charles Horner. Unidentified men pose with their trophies (below) at a hunting club in Green Bank. (Above, courtesy of the New Egypt Historical Society; below, courtesy of Budd Wilson.)

Decoy carving was another popular activity in the Pine Barrens. Jack Updike was one of several skilled carvers in the area. When asked his secret, he replied, "All I know is, you got to be plenty smart to fool a duck." (Photograph by William F. Augustine; courtesy of Pete Stemmer.)

The sneakbox was a 12- to 15-foot sailboat designed by Hazelton Seaman of West Creek around 1836. As the name implies, it was used for sneaking up on ducks, geese, and other birds. Known for making sneakboxes, Sam Hunt (right) of Waretown explains his work to researcher George Petty. (Courtesy of Ocean County Cultural and Heritage Commission.)

Most people think of the woods when they think of the Pine Barrens, but parts of it touch the bay. Norman Dupont, who was born in Waretown in 1928, said, "In those days there were two ways to make a living and that was either you go on the water or work in the woods. I done them all one time or another." Above, some clammers fill their sneakboxes with the day's catch. Below, pound fishermen are bringing in the results of their labor. (Both, courtesy of Ocean County Cultural and Heritage Commission.)

Clamming was often a way of life for the baymen. Over 100 years ago, James P. Ward of West Creek wrote this about the baymen: "He thoroughly understands the various modes of catching clam; sometimes he is seen tonging, and at other times raking and during the long summer days when the tides are low he may be seen diving for them." In the 1940s, the going rate was 80¢ per 100 clams. In the mid-1900s, a bayman could pull 2,500 clams out of the water in a day, but the supply is no longer plentiful, and clam replenishment programs are underway in the area, particularly around Barnegat Bay. (Both, courtesy of Ocean County Cultural and Heritage Commission.)

Blacksmiths and wheelwrights were vital members of a 19th-century village. Horses needed shoes, axes needed sharpening, and houses needed hinges and latches. Prior to the 19th century, some blacksmiths would make nails by inserting a pointed bit of hot iron rod into a nail header and hammering it with glancing blows until a head was formed. Blacksmith Fish is seen in his shop (right) around 1905. Wheelwrights, like the gentleman shown below, made and repaired wagons and wheels. (Right, courtesy of the Burlington County Historical Society; below, courtesy of the Lighthouse Tavern.)

Itinerant blacksmiths were common, taking their needed equipment on the road with them as they went to farms and villages. Horses that were ridden or used for work needed their hooves trimmed and horseshoes put on to protect their feet from the extra strain placed on them. (Both, courtesy of the New Jersey Forest Service.)

Four
PEOPLE AND PLACES

James Still was born in 1812 in a Medford log cabin. His parents, Levin and Charity Still, were former slaves. Still only had three months of formal schooling and taught himself herbal remedies from books on medical botany he purchased. Patients came from all over to receive treatments from Still, who was known as The Black Doctor of the Pines. (Courtesy of the Burlington County Historical Society.)

Dr. James Still became the wealthiest landowner in the Medford area at the time from his unlicensed medical practice. Above is Dr. Still's residence; his office is seen at the left in the illustration. The Victorian house was demolished in 1932. The office was built in the 1850s and later remodeled. The office and 8-acre parcel were purchased in 2010 by the Department of Environmental Protection to preserve this site, which was listed on both the New Jersey and National Registers of Historic Places in 1995. Below is the hospital Still worked at. (Both, courtesy of the Burlington County Historical Society.)

Benjamin O. Wade had a general store and residence built in 1865, on the corner of First and Main Streets in Chatsworth, known as "The Capital of the Pines." Main Street later became Route 563. Wade ran the store for 32 years then sold it to Willis Jefferson Buzby in 1897. (Courtesy of R. Marilyn Schmidt.)

Buzby's General Store offered staples like flour and coffee as well as penny candy, shotgun shells, and Esso gasoline. Author Henry Charlton Beck said that Buzby always had "ready advice on law, etiquette, investments, medicine and religion." (Courtesy of R. Marilyn Schmidt.)

Buzby's son, Willis Jonathan Buzby, inherited the property after his father's death. He married the girl next door, Katie Ritzendollar, and they were soon known as the "King and Queen of the Pineys." As a wedding present, they received Katie's grandmother's former house, across the street from the store. (Courtesy of R. Marilyn Schmidt.)

Prince Volupi Ruspoli was born in this house in what was once Union Forge, named for an old forge run by William Cook around 1800. Thomas and Samuel Richards originally established the forge for the manufacture of pig iron, which was fashioned into bar iron. By 1932, nothing remained. The town was renamed Shamong Station when the railroad came in 1859, and today is called Chatsworth. (Courtesy of the Burlington County Library.)

Post offices were usually in homes or general stores in the 1800s and early 1900s. The William Johnson home in Lower Bank (above) served as both a store and a post office. When Charles Landis set out to establish Vineland, he had trouble convincing the Postmaster General to permit a post office there because there were not any inhabitants yet. In those days, only settlements of sufficient importance warranted the location of a post office. The Steelmanville general store and stagecoach stop (below) was also used as a post office from 1875 until 1913. (Above, courtesy of Budd Wilson; below, courtesy of the Atlantic County Historical Society.)

Born Ann Ashatama near the Forks of the Rancocas Creek, Indian Ann was the last full-blooded Delaware Indian in New Jersey; she died in 1894 at the age of 90. Ann followed in her family's basketmaking footsteps and regularly sold her handmade wares in Medford and Vincentown. Her baskets, like the one shown below, are treasured heirlooms, and some can be seen at the Shamong Municipal Building. Ann married John Roberts and had seven children. She lived at one point in a one-room log cabin (above) on Dingletown Road in Indian Mills. (Above, courtesy of the Burlington County Historical Society; below, courtesy of Pola Galie.)

Lila W. Thompson (right) was born on March 9, 1875, in New Egypt. She married Joseph Thompson in 1891 at the age of 16, and together they had three sons. After women gained the right to vote, Lila became active in politics. She ran for Ocean County's only assembly seat and won by 1,630 votes, becoming the first woman to represent an entire county in the state legislature. She was easily reelected in 1924, but she vacated her seat to run for the Senate. She was defeated by her opponent, Thomas Mathis, and withdrew from politics. In 1931, she was selected as the first director of the Ocean County Old Age Pension Relief Bureau. This 1925 image (below) shows, from left to right, (first row) Pres. Calvin Coolidge, unidentified, Lila Thompson, and New Jersey governor Walter Edge. (Both, courtesy of the New Egypt Historical Society.)

While the country was in the throes of the Great Depression in 1929, George Daynor believed he found a cure. For $4, he purchased 4 acres of swampland in Vineland that had been used as an automobile dumping ground and proceeded to turn the property into Depression Palace. Working over a three-year period, he used automobile parts, rocks, and whatever else he could find to build an 18-turret castle that was visited by 250,000 people before it was razed in the 1960s. Daynor believed there was no reason for people not to be able to find work and make money. Building the castle must have lifted the spirits of Daynor (below), as he lived to the ripe old age of 104. (Both, courtesy of the Cumberland County Historical Society.)

Betty Jane Crowley grew up in Green Bank and was crowned Miss New Jersey 1949. Under the stage name Kathleen Crowley, she acted in movies and television, including *A Star is Born*, *Jane Eyre*, *Bonanza*, *Thriller*, *The Virginian*, *77 Sunset Strip*, *Batman*, and many others. This photograph is autographed to her cousin, the late Marilyn Browne Wilson. (Courtesy of Budd Wilson.)

Capt. Charles "Budd" Wilson was a mounted state trooper in the Chatsworth area during the 1920s. He would ride 30 miles from the Troop A barracks in Hammonton. Wilson later became the chief of the Delaware River Port Authority Police and was instrumental in helping Arthur Pierce with historical research and the daybooks from Batsto. (Courtesy of Budd Wilson.)

Steelmantown originated in the early 1700s. In 1842, Hezekiah Creamer sold land for a schoolhouse, church, and cemetery. The original Steelman/Creamer burial ground is now Steelmantown Cemetery, a green cemetery using only natural burying methods. It is the only cemetery in New Jersey certified and approved by the Green Burial Council as a Level 3 natural burial ground. (Photograph by author.)

One-room schoolhouses dotted the Pine Barrens. This is the original Indian Mills schoolhouse, which was replaced with a more modern building in 1910. The new school would be burned while being used as a Prohibition still. (Photograph by Nathaniel R. Ewan; courtesy of Burlington County Historical Society.)

The Cedar Crest School was located on the second floor of Beam's General Store, which also served as the Bamber post office. These unidentified children arrived by a horse-drawn "school bus" (above). The Wading River School's students in this c. 1915 photograph (below) include, from left to right, (first row) Orville McAnney, Kenneth Bozarth, Isaac Maxwell, Elsie McAnney, Lemuel Maxwell, Susie Maxwell, and unidentified; (second row) teacher Miss Weeks, Elizabeth Maxwell, Allie Lippincott, Mary McAnney, Beatrice McAnney, Myrtle Lippincott, and Glada Downs; (third row) Stanley Downs, Wilbur Lippincott, Matthew Maxwell, Charles Lippincott, and Lewis Maxwell. Weeks's right arm had been amputated at the elbow. (Above, courtesy of the Lacey Township Historical Society; below, courtesy of Budd Wilson.)

Elizabeth Meirs Morgan was a well-known historian and naturalist, who did much to help conserve sections of land in and around the Pine Barrens that she loved so much. She was born in New Egypt, near the Stone Hills that are part of the Coastal Divide, and died at the age of 90 in Forked River. She had a master's degree in history and worked as a teacher and social worker. (Photograph by Luke Pelligra; courtesy of Pola Galie.)

This donkey-drawn trolley was used at the Vineland Training School for Feeble-Minded Girls and Boys. Elizabeth Kite worked at this school, and it was here that she wrote her famous study in 1912 based on a fictitious family she named Kallikak, a combination of the Greek words for good and evil. This falsified study spawned the word *Piney* to describe people she portrayed as promiscuous, inbred, and drunkards. (Courtesy of the Vineland Historical Society.)

According to the U.S. Trotting Association, Stanley Dancer was the only horseman to drive and train three Triple Crown of Harness Racing winners—Nevele Pride in 1968 for trotting, Most Happy Fella in 1970 for pacing, and Super Bowl in 1972 for trotting. Dancer won his first race at age 17 and continued to train and drive for 50 years. He drove winners in 23 Triple Crown races, a record that stood for 20 years; trained five Hambletonian winners; and guided four Little Brown Jug champions. He earned his 3,781st and last win as a driver in 1995 at Garden State Park. He and his wife, Rachel, hosted the New Jersey Sire Stakes for several years at their home, Egyptian Acres, in New Egypt. (Both, courtesy of the New Egypt Historical Society.)

This beautiful panorama of Lower Bank looking northwest towards Green Bank was taken around the beginning of the 20th century. River Road cuts through the picture, connecting with Batsto/Bridgeport Road (also known as Route 542) on the right. At the end of this road, partially obscured by trees and the house in front, is the Lower Bank School, which was moved to Smithville. The barn seen in the lower right corner belonged to Capt. Jesse Reuben Cavileer and his wife, Nettie.

He later built the Victorian house seen in the center foreground and converted his former residence into a barn. The Victorian home was struck by lightning and burned down, causing the Cavileers to convert the barn back into a home. It later burned down. The house on the left was owned by George Maxwell and is no longer standing. (Courtesy of Budd Wilson.)

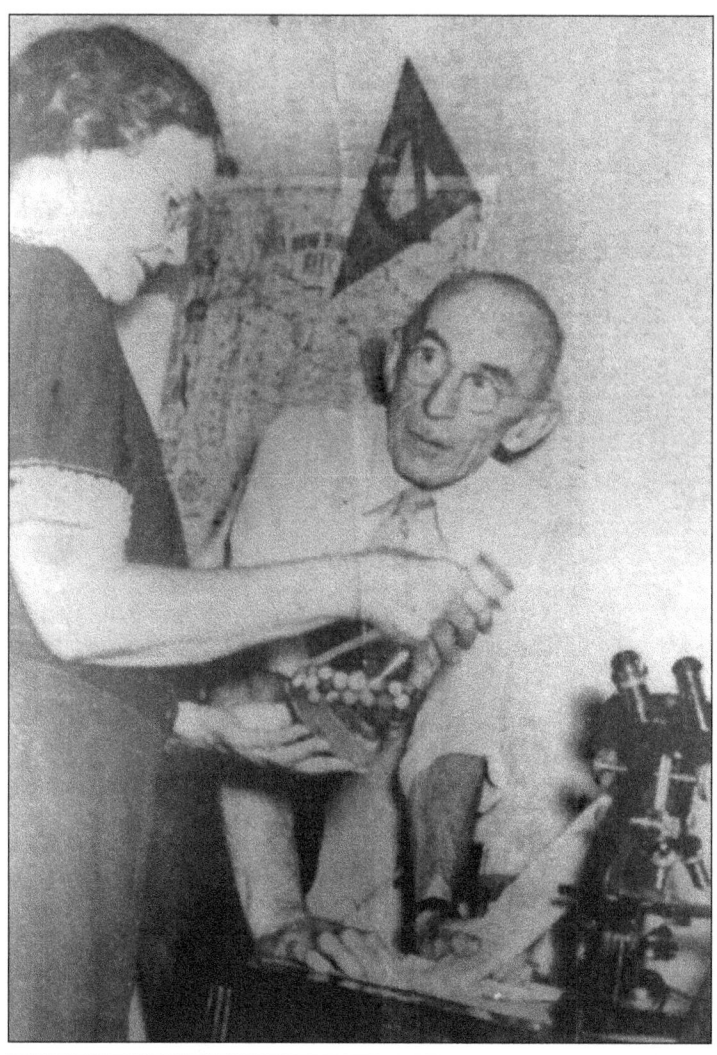

Elizabeth Lee (left) owned acres of cranberry bogs with her brother, Enoch Bills, on what is now called Cranberry Canners Lane in New Egypt. One day, instead of throwing out some damaged cranberries, she decided to boil them instead with some sugar, and the rest is history. She liked the taste; started canning it, and the world's first canned cranberry sauce was made available. Her recipe was so popular that the family had to build a canning factory (below). Selling product under the name Bog Sweet Cranberry Sauce, the company later became part of Ocean Spray. (Both, courtesy of the New Egypt Historical Society.)

Five

RAILS

On February 21, 1929, the pride of the Central Railroad of New Jersey's fleet, the *Blue Comet*, came to life. It was billed as the "Seashore's Finest Train" and took passengers from Jersey City to Atlantic City in three hours. The *Blue Comet* service was initially assigned three refurbished G3 Pacific locomotives with whistles that came from steamboats on the Mississippi River. (Courtesy of the Ocean County Cultural and Heritage Commission.)

The cars of the Blue Comet were painted Packard Blue for the sky, Royal Blue for the sea, and along their sides, Jersey Cream for the sandy beaches. On the glass was an etched design of a comet, stars, and clouds. The observation cars were furnished with two rows of 24 silver blue reed armchairs upholstered in blue plush and blue carpets with a comet design in gold. The train ran on schedule 97 percent of the time. But on August 19, 1939, the Chatsworth Cranberry Company reported 13.5 inches of rain, which washed out the roadbed at a culvert three miles south of Chatsworth, causing the tracks to drop several inches. This resulted in the *Blue Comet's* only mishap in its history (above and below). Out of 49 passengers, only three were seriously injured. (Both, photographs by J. Edward Jaques; courtesy of Frank Ingram.)

Record rainfall was not just affecting Chatsworth. Problems were reported throughout the state. A 15-inch rain gauge at the Sterling Otis bogs in Tuckerton overflowed. In the photograph above, New Jersey Route 4 in Tuckerton (present day Route 9) lies under 18 inches of water. The sign for Tuckerton Creek normally pertained to the body of water to the right of the guardrail and below the overpass, but in this storm, the placement seemed very appropriate. As seen in the bottom photograph, more than 750 feet of sidewalk was torn off and washed into the creek. Trees were uprooted, and numerous building foundations and automobiles were damaged. (Both, courtesy of the Tuckerton Historical Society.)

In Herman City, the Johnson sawmill washed out for the last time. John Pearce reported that every dam in the area had washed out during the August 1939 record rainfall as well as many of the bridges. The sawmill was originally built by Nicolas Sooy II around 1803, along with a grist mill. It had washed out in 1903 and was rebuilt, but this time it met its demise. (Courtesy of Budd Wilson.)

Even though it was the geographical center of the state, New Egypt remained isolated until the Pemberton and Hightstown Railroad arrived on February 6, 1868. When they stopped the line, the Union Transportation Company was formed to operate a train between Pemberton and Hightstown. In the early 1900s, trains helped make New Egypt a resort town, with the summer population swelling to more than 10,000. (Courtesy of the New Egypt Historical Society.)

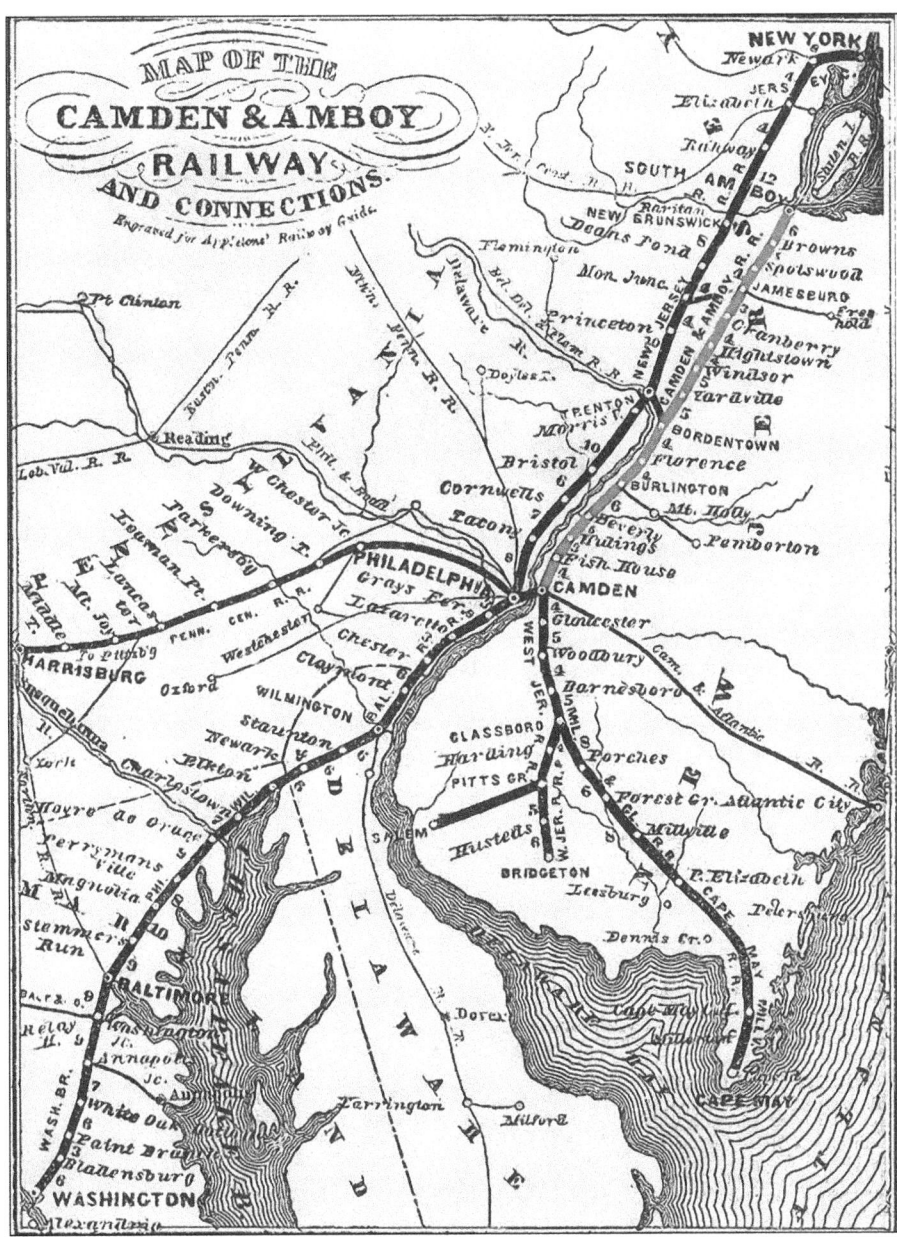

The first railroad legislation in the United States was signed into law on February 6, 1815. This act, which had a 10-year limit, was the brainchild of Col. John Stevens, who wanted "to erect a railroad from the River Delaware, near Trenton, to the River Raritan, at or near New Brunswick." Later, the Camden and Amboy Railroad and Transportation Company and the Delaware and Raritan Canal Company were both chartered by the New Jersey legislature on February 4, 1830. Given that the 1815 act had become null and void, the organizers of the Camden and Amboy had to start anew. The two companies were joined by an act of union on February 15, 1831, and on March 2, 1832, were given protection by another act of the state legislature that no other company could build a rail line between New York and Philadelphia, essentially creating a monopoly. The Camden and Amboy would go on to operate the first locomotive in New Jersey. (Courtesy of Appletons' Railway and Steam Navigation Guide.)

On November 12, 1831, *John Bull* executed the first movement by steam on a railroad in New Jersey. Made in Britain, it was purchased by Robert Stevens for the Camden and Amboy Railroad. It was given the number 1 and the name *Stevens* but was more commonly known as *John Bull*. It is the oldest operable steam locomotive in North America. The later version pictured here was photographed about 1893. (Courtesy of the Library of Congress.)

This Mogul-class locomotive, so named due to its 2-6-0 wheel arrangement, is pictured near the Liverpool Avenue crossing in Egg Harbor City. This engine, built by a predecessor of the Baldwin Locomotive Works in May 1901, was purchased new by the West Jersey and Seashore Railroad. The West Jersey and Seashore was controlled by the Pennsylvania Railroad, which spent nearly 50 years competing with the Reading Railroad for the lucrative seashore traffic in South Jersey. (Courtesy of Mark W. Maxwell.)

Between 1864 and 1931, the Raritan and Delaware Bay Railroad Company (R&DB) engine house was in Lakehurst. The R&DB was chartered in March 1854 to construct a railroad from Raritan Bay to Cape May. Instead of heading southeast from Lakehurst to Cape May, the line was diverted southwest to Atsion in 1862. It joined forces with the Camden and Atlantic Railroad to form a connecting line between Atsion and Atco, providing service between New York and Philadelphia. This challenged the state authorized monopoly of the Camden and Amboy Railroad, which took the matter to court. The R&DB lost and filed bankruptcy; it reorganized in 1869 as the New Jersey Southern Railroad. The R&DB opened a branch to Toms River in 1866, which continued to the Waretown station (below) in 1872. (Above, courtesy of the Ocean County Cultural and Heritage Commission; below, courtesy of the Lighthouse Tavern.)

The Tuckerton Railroad Company, Time Table No. 219, Effective September 29, 1935

Week Days	EASTERN STANDARD TIME		Week Days
Train 11 P.M.			Train 10 A.M.
	Lv. Beach Haven .... (P.& B.H.R.R.) Ar.		
	" North Beach Haven	"	
	" Spray Beach	"	
	" Beach Haven Terrace	"	
	" Peahala (Brighton Beach)	"	
	" Beach Haven Crest	"	
	" Brant Beach	"	
	" Ship Bottom-Beach Arlington	"	
	" Hilliard	"	
	Ar. Manahawken	Lv.	
2.22	Lv. Tuckerton .... (T.R.R.) Ar.		11.02
f 2.27	" Parkertown	Lv.	f 10.57
f 2.29	" West Creek	"	f 10.55
f 2.32	" Cox Station	"	f 10.51
f 2.37	" Staffordville	"	f 10.46
f 2.41	" Mayetta	"	f 10.42
f 2.43	" Cedar Run	"	f 10.40
2.47	Ar. Manahawken		10.33
2.52	Lv. Manahawken	Ar.	10.28
3.04	" Barnegat	Lv.	10.18
f 3.07	" Waretown Jct.	"	f 10.10
	" Lacy	"	
f 3.29	" Cedar Crest	"	f 9.53
3.44	Ar. Whitings	"	9.45
3.59	Lv. Whitings (P.R.R.)	Ar.	9.40
4.40	Ar. Mt. Holly	Lv.	8.55
5.27	" Camden	" "	8.13
5.35	" Philadelphia (Market St.)	" "	8.05
h 5.45	Ar. Trenton	Lv.	x 3.44
h 6.46	" Newark (Penna. Sta.)	" "	2.52
h 7.02	" Jersey City (Journal Sq.)	" "	2.09
h 7.11	" New York (Hudson Ter'l)	" "	2.00
h 7.10	" New York (Penna. Sta.)	" "	2.35
	Lv. Whitings .... (C.R.R. of N.J.) Ar.		7.55
	Ar. Lakehurst	Lv.	7.40
c 6.04	" Lakewood	" "	7.15
c 6.30	" Red Bank	" "	6.15
c 7.21	" Jersey City	" "	3.32
c 7.33	" New York (Liberty St.)	" "	3.00
c 7.47	" New York (W. 23rd St.)	" "	
P.M.			A.M.

(Left margin: Via Birmingham; Right margin: Via Broad St., Philadelphia)

INFORMATION: This railroad is not responsible for errors in time tables, inconvenience or damage resulting from delayed trains or failure to make connections; schedules herein are subject to change without notice.

NOTES: "f" Indicates Flag stations. Stops only on signal or notice to Agent or Conductor to receive or discharge passengers.
"c" Via Barnegat and Motor Coach.
"h" Connection does not run Nov. 28, Dec. 25, Jan. 1 or Feb. 22
"x" Connection from Trenton only except on Nov. 28, Dec. 25, Jan. 1 and Feb. 22, via Birmingham leaves 6.45 A. M.

On March 22, 1866, the Barnegat Railroad Company was chartered by a legislative act to build a line from what is now Lakehurst to Manahawkin, with the option to go to Tuckerton. On March 31, 1869, the name changed to the Manchester and Barnegat Bay Railway Company, which could build to Lakehurst or Toms River. A third amendment on March 14, 1870, allowed the railroad to build from any point on the New Jersey Southern Railroad within Ocean County. Finally a fourth amendment was approved on February 15, 1871, changing the name to the Tuckerton Railroad. At its apex, the system stretched from Whitings to Manahawkin and to Tuckerton, Beach Haven, and Barnegat City. In October 1939, the owners filed for abandonment. The rails were removed in 1940. This 1935 timetable shows different spellings of certain stations: Manahawken (now Manahawkin), Lacy (Lacey), and Whitings (Whiting). (Courtesy of the Ocean County Cultural and Heritage Commission.)

The Tuckerton Railroad passed through a remote area of Lacey Township in its travels between Whitings and Tuckerton. Tiny stations were located at Middle Branch, Lacy, and Bamber, where a southbound "mixed" train No. 10, pulled by locomotive No. 6 with a borrowed combine and two boxcars in tow, runs alongside present-day Lacey Road after leaving the station in August 1933. Its last run was on January 31, 1936. (Courtesy of the Lacey Township Historical Society.)

Tuckerton also had an old gallows-type merry-go-round. The turntable was a 52-foot long Armstrong. The engine is a No. 4 (wheel arrangement 4-4-0) built by Baldwin in 1890. It burned anthracite coal. Seen with the engine are, from left to right, Samuel Marshall, Arthur Horner, and William Malsbury. (Photograph by Chester Pharo; courtesy of the Ocean County Cultural and Heritage Commission.)

This is the Browns Mills branch terminus of the Philadelphia and Long Branch Railroad, which merged with the Pemberton and Seashore Railroad in 1883. In 1925, the Pennsylvania Railroad, which controlled this line, filed with the state to abandon the Browns Mills and Burlington branches, which was approved. This terminus was demolished and the tracks removed that same year. (Photograph by Nathaniel R. Ewan; courtesy of the Burlington County Historical Society.)

The Vincentown branch of the Camden and Amboy Railroad was incorporated in March 1860. The line was extended to the pits of the Vincentown Marl Company in 1866. Marl is being loaded onto the gondola cars in this c. 1867 photograph. Gen. John S. Irick, president of the railroad, is shown in foreground. Col. Timothy Bryan is shown just off to the rear. (Courtesy of the Burlington County Historical Society.)

In 1955, Rev. Charlie Ashmen and his wife, Nellie, envisioned a Christian camp on 114 acres of abandoned cranberry bogs in Winslow Township. That vision became Haluwasa, an acronym for Charlie's favorite hymn, "Hallelujah, What a Savior." The property was rich in sand and gravel, used to build the rail beds for Haluwasa's three-mile, 24-gauge railroad, the country's longest. The $12,000 price tag for a steam engine was too high, so Charlie bought parts and built one. A mechanic's son, he was a marine machinist in World War II and put this knowledge to use, adapting an air-pressurized windshield wiper to power the bell and Jeep Rambler differentials to run the wheels. As Charlie put it, "There's something about a train that brings out the child in all of us." (Both, courtesy of the Ashmen family.)

Cities like Hammonton, Atlantic City, and Egg Harbor City owe their existence to the Camden and Atlantic Railroad. During its inaugural trip on July 1, 1854, several German businessmen viewed the surrounding area and envisioned the establishment of a German community. When the German Americans started arriving in Egg Harbor City in September 1855, it may have been the largest influx of settlers in the Pine Barrens up until that time. The Camden and Atlantic Railroad offered six months of free travel on the line to anyone who built a home valued at $300 or more in the settlement. Pictured above is the West Jersey and Seashore Railroad station in Egg Harbor City around 1905. Below, presidential candidate Theodore Roosevelt made a stop at Liverpool Avenue in Egg Harbor City in 1912. (Both, courtesy of the Egg Harbor City Historical Society.)

Six
Proud to be a Piney

The Jersey Devil could be called the Pine Barrens unofficial mascot. Legend has it that he was born to a woman named Leeds in 1735 in the town of Leeds Point. She had 12 children already and cursed the baby during childbirth, saying, "Let him be a devil!" At birth, the baby reputedly sprouted wings, tail, and claws and flew out into the Pine Barrens, where he has lived ever since. (Courtesy of the Tuckerton Historical Society.)

On southbound Route 539, about six miles north of the Route 72 intersection, sits a brightly painted five-foot-by-seven-foot boulder. For years, Edward Gillesheimer, a retiree who lives nearby, painted different designs to match the seasons. But since 9/11, the rock has proudly and steadfastly worn a painted American flag, with stands of American flags adorning it on either side. (Photograph by author.)

The Pygmy Pines, or The Plains, as this section has been called, is a curiosity in nature. Mature pitch pines and oaks fill this area by Warren Grove, but most are not even five feet tall. From certain spots of the road, you can see for miles over these treetops. The cause of this dwarfism is unknown, although frequent fires in this area may be the reason. (Courtesy of Pete Stemmer.)

Many towns in the Pine Barrens have interesting names—with even more interesting stories about the origins of names like Good Luck, Double Trouble, Chicken Bone, and many more. The basis for the name of Ong's Hat (right) is uncertain, but a popular legend is that a young man named Ong had a disagreement with his girlfriend, became enraged, tossed his hat into a high tree, and there it stayed. The origin of Bargaintown (below) is also uncertain, but the town's favorite legend centers around James Somers, who made a bargain with his slaves that if they would build a bridge across Patcong Creek, he would give them their freedom and a piece of land. They built Cedar Swamp Bridge, and Somers honored his bargain. (Right, courtesy of the New Jersey Forest Service; below, courtesy of the Greate Egg Harbour Historical Society.)

A banjo, a dulcimer, even a washboard and tub can coax foot-stamping and applause from the audience at Albert Music Hall. Almost every Saturday night, the music of the pines still wafts through Waretown, as it did so many years ago. The Albert brothers—George, (left) and Joe (below)—lived in a cabin in Waretown affectionately known as the Home Place. On Saturday evenings, friends would drop by, bring their instruments to pick, and all would sing until the wee hours of the morning. There was no electricity in the cabin, but some gas lights and homemade coffee and cake kept the place warm and glowing. The Home Place became widely known, and soon hundreds of people were coming to listen to the impromptu sessions. (Both, courtesy of the Pinelands Cultural Society.)

An aerial view of the Home Place is shown above. When George Albert, who played the fiddle, died, his brother found it hard to handle the growing crowds alone, and so the music stopped . . . for six months. Then some musicians got together, rented a room at the Waretown auction, charged the public a small fee, and the "Sounds of the Jersey Pines" were heard again. This was the formation of the Pinelands Cultural Society. When the auction building was destroyed by fire in July 1992, the pickers continued to gather in the parking lot. Today, Albert Music Hall has a permanent home where musicians like Jim Murphy and the Pine Barons (below) can play while interacting with faithful audiences. A "pickin' shed" next door allows for impromptu sessions, encouragement, and great music. (Both, courtesy of the Pinelands Cultural Society.)

Snapper soup can be found on the menu of many restaurants in and around the Pine Barrens. As a way to earn money, boys in the Pines would often catch snapping turtles to sell to restaurants. Snappers are voracious eaters and can be quite aggressive on land. Their serpentine necks can stretch rather far, and their jaws are powerful enough to amputate a finger. (Courtesy of Edward F. Bixby II.)

The northern pine snake (*Pituophis melanoleucus melanoleucus*) is New Jersey's only threatened snake species. Its length is from 48 to 66 inches long, with dark patches on light-colored skin. The snake's habitat is limited to the Pine Barrens, as it prefers the sandy soil. Charles Barnett of Egg Harbor Township is holding up two of the snakes he found. (Courtesy of the Greate Egg Harbour Historical Society.)

Outhouses once dotted the backyards of homes throughout the Pine Barrens (as well as elsewhere in America), and many in the Pines continued to rely on them into the end of the 20th century. Locals said that Buzby's store in Chatsworth was the cleanest one in town, and it always had a white lace curtain in the window. (Courtesy of photographer Andrew Gioulis.)

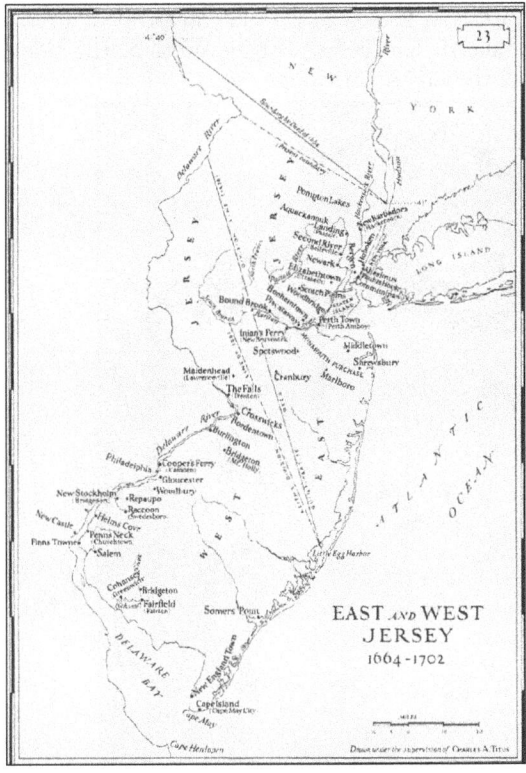

In 1644, the Duke of York gave the colony of New Jersey to Lord John Berkeley and Sir George Carteret. They split it into two provinces, East Jersey and West Jersey, using a line drawn by surveyor George Keith, which became known as the Keith Line. Disputes led to another survey and a different line, this one called the Lawrence Line. (Courtesy of the Ocean County Cultural and Heritage Commission.)

Built around 1740, the Cedar Bridge Tavern (above) sits between the Keith and Lawrence lines dividing the Province of New Jersey into East Jersey and West Jersey. The last documented land engagement of the Revolutionary War took place here. After official hostilities waned, some Loyalists took refuge in the Pine Barrens, among them Capt. John Bacon. Capt. Richard Shreve set out to find Bacon and encountered him by the Cedar Bridge Tavern. Bacon escaped but was later captured and killed near Parkertown. The tavern's bar (below) is believed to be the oldest original intact bar in America. (Both, courtesy of the Library of Congress.)

One religion actually began here: Lanoka Harbor is considered the birthplace of Universalism. In 1760, the area was known as Good Luck. Thomas Potter, a fisherman, farmer, and religious man, built Potter Church (above) as a nondenominational house of worship. Quakers, Presbyterians, Baptists, and Methodists all preached here. On July 21, 1770, the Rev. John Murray preached the first Universalist sermon in America. Another unique ceremony has been held in the Pines since the 1960s. The United Methodist Church in Warren Grove (below) conducts a deer hunters service the night before shotgun hunting season starts. Rev. Barry Steinmetz is the current pastor. (Above, courtesy of the Lacey Township Historical Society; below, photograph by author.)

Fires burn hotter and faster in the Pine Barrens than anywhere in America, according to retired Pine Barrens forest fire warden Jeff Brower. A fire in the western states may burn 10,000 acres in three days, but in the Pine Barrens, that same acreage can burn in three hours. State geologists believe that 70,000 to 100,000 acres burned annually in the Pines in the late 1800s. Today about 1,600 wildfires erupt each year throughout New Jersey. Above, a member of the New Jersey Forest Fire Service is at the scene of a fire in the Pine Barrens. Below, Victor Bush of Pemberton stands alongside his firefighting wagon in 1911. (Above, courtesy of the New Jersey Forest Fire Service; below, courtesy of the New Jersey Forest Service.)

The fire ecology of the Pine Barrens is what keeps the area from becoming the "Oak Barrens" instead. Oaks are taller trees that would eventually crowd out the pitch pines, the predominant pine tree in the area. But oaks cannot withstand intense fires, whereas the dark, thick-scaled bark of a pitch pine protects it from the heat. Pinecones also need the heat to melt the resin and allow the seeds to open so that new trees can be propagated. Within weeks of a blaze, new growth is seen on the blackened pitch pines. Lookout towers help with quick detection of wildfires. The Four Mile tower was a simple tripod constructed in 1910. (Courtesy of the New Jersey Forest Service.)

Apple Pie Hill is the highest point in the Pine Barrens. The image at left shows an early version of the Apple Pie Hill fire tower. (Courtesy of the Burlington County Historical Society.)

In the 1930s, Rev. Henry Charlton Beck was a reporter for the *Courier Post of Camden* when he started visiting forgotten towns in Southern New Jersey and interviewing the people he met there. Those interviews spawned a series of books on the area. Although his work has been criticized over the years for not always being accurate, Beck was the first person to bring the people of the Pine Barrens to the public's attention. In the image above, Beck (left) talks with an unidentified man (center) and Jay C. Parker of Tuckerton. John McPhee spotlighted the area 30 years later in his book, *The Pine Barrens*. He told stories of the Pineys, mainly through two characters, Fred Brown and Bill Wasovwich, the latter shown standing (left) in front of a wood pile he split by hand. (Above, courtesy of the Tuckerton Seaport; left, courtesy of photographer Andrew Gioulis.)

Seven
GONE BUT NOT FORGOTTEN

In 1943, the United States Navy took over land owned by the estate of Henry Phipps on Island Beach for the purpose of developing a missile program. A team fashioned the world's first ramjet from the exhaust pipe of a P-47 Thunderbolt fighter plane. The "flying stovepipe," as it was nicknamed, was launched on June 13, 1945, and traveled at a speed of 1,500 miles per hour. (Courtesy of the Ocean County Cultural and Heritage Commission.)

In 1944, a launching pad was erected on the sand dunes of Island Beach. Operating under the code name Bumblebee, 30 highly trained scientists from John Hopkins University's Applied Physics Laboratory were brought in to experiment with the world's first supersonic antiaircraft guided missile system. The missiles were propelled on a southeast course, allowing them to splash down in the Atlantic Ocean. (Courtesy of the Ocean County Cultural and Heritage Commission.)

A typical colonial house in the 1700s would have a spinning wheel near the hearth. Many unmarried woman spent time spinning wool for the family and were known as spinsters. This was considered an important, patriotic role, like men going off to war. As she spun, she would tell stories, and this is where the term "spinning a yarn" comes from. (Courtesy of the Cumberland County Historical Society.)

The town of Amatol, which is named after one of the explosives used in the plant, occupied about 350 acres. Like Belcoville, this was a planned community to support a World War I munitions plant. It was designed to maintain a population of 25,000 and included a railroad, heating plant, laundry, woodworking shop, dormitories like the one seen above, and several commercial structures. Construction on the plant began March 4, 1918, and two miles away—to protect the people in case of an explosion—work began on the town of Amatol as well. Even though the town was erected quickly, the focus was on its general attractiveness, with symmetry and planned garden areas, like the one at Liberty Court (below). (Above, courtesy of Bernard Graebener; below, courtesy of Atlantic County Historical Society.)

The Atlantic City Raceway was built in 1926 on a portion of the former Amatol site and has been called the "Amatol Racetrack." Built at a cost of $1 million and sponsored by Charles M. Schwab, Marshall R. Ward, H. E. Clark, and S. D. Clark, the steeply banked, 1.5-mile-long, and 50-foot-wide oval was built to handle speeds of 160 miles per hour. At the time, it was billed as "the fastest board track in the country." For a short time, it was rated better than the Indianapolis 500 track. The grandstand could hold 60,000 people, and at the time, 20 percent of the population of the United States was located within 150 miles of the raceway. (Both, courtesy of Bernard Graebener.)

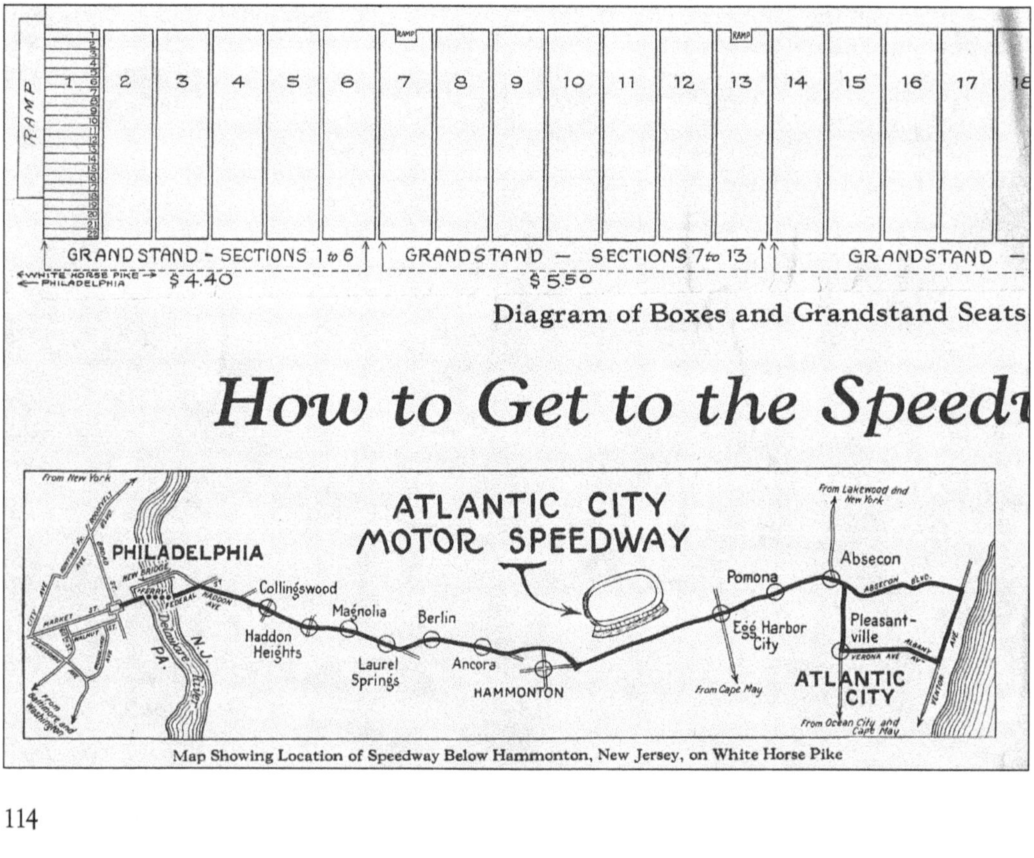

This is an overview of the Atlantic City Raceway in 1926. Two cars are racing on the track at the very bottom. The grandstand and parking lot are in the center, and the dark oval in the top half of the photograph is actually a train. (Courtesy of Bernard Graebener.)

Dr. Smith believed that cedar water from the serpentine creek (at left) would "revitalize the body and cure its ills." So he built Dr. Smith's Neutral Water Health Resort Sanitarium in Egg Harbor City and encouraged people to walk in the creek. The Roundhouse Museum is seen in the foreground. (Courtesy of the Egg Harbor City Historical Society.)

The Chatsworth Clubhouse was essentially a millionaire's resort, located on the banks of the old Union Forge Lake. Union Forge was an area in Burlington County named for the forge operated by William Cook around 1800. Around 1859, the railroad came into this area and the town was renamed Shamong Station. Today, it is called Chatsworth. The clubhouse was in full operation around 1890, and these photographs of the exterior and interior were taken about 1895. One of the presidents of the clubhouse was Levi Morton, former vice president of the United States. The clubhouse was said to be "elaborately fitted" and hosted many famous dinners and "social affairs of New York's high society." It burned down around 1910. (Both, courtesy of the Burlington County Library.)

Game farms were a new concept in this country when the New Jersey Fish and Game Commission purchased property from Charles A. Smith in the early 1900s for $4,000. The commission felt the salt meadow surrounded by briars and underbrush would be an ideal cover for the English pheasants, wild turkey, quail, and deer it was planning to raise for hunting. The original farmhouse on the property (below), with sections dating back to 1784, was renovated by the state and used by the gamekeeper. The commission purchased additional acreage, and soon the Forked River Game Farm (above) consisted of 600 acres. It raised 6,500 pheasants in 1919 and set approximately 12,000 eggs. Over the years, the game farm flourished until the commission closed it in 1983, feeling it was more cost effective to buy pheasants than to raise them. (Both, courtesy of the Lacey Township Historical Society.)

On April 15, 1865, Sarah McKeen, Hannah Prince, and Hess Rake had just finished sewing an American flag to commemorate the end of the Civil War when news of President Lincoln's assassination arrived. They sewed three vertical black stripes onto the flag as symbols of mourning and hung the flag in front of the McKeen Hotel. On July 4, 1920, from left to right, McKeen's great-grandniece, Martina Adams; Martha Merchant; and Samuel Merchant stand beneath that same flag at Samuel and Martha Merchant's gas station. (Courtesy of Lee Eichinger.)

Some residents still recall the sight of low-flying airships heading towards the Lakehurst Naval Station. But such views ended after May 6, 1937, when the German passenger airship *Hindenburg* caught fire as it attempted to dock at the base. In addition to one ground fatality, 35 people on board died. (Courtesy of the Ocean County Cultural and Heritage Commission.)

Capt. Emilio Carranza was known as the "Mexican Lindbergh." He became a national hero when he was chosen to undertake a goodwill flight from Mexico City to New York City in response to the same flight undertaken by Lindbergh in 1927. He arrived safely but encountered a thunderstorm on the return trip and died in a crash in the Pine Barrens in July 1928. Historian Alice Weber stands next to the monument that marks the crash site. (Photograph by Burrel Adams; courtesy of Pete Stemmer.)

The Bear Swamp Hill fire tower was a favorite spot of Alice Weber and others to overlook the Pine Barrens. In 1971, it was struck by an F-105 Thunderchief during a routine bombing run. Fortunately, no one was in the tower at the time, but the pilot died and the crash destroyed the tower and numerous trees. The tower was not rebuilt. (Courtesy of Steve Eichinger.)

Belcoville's history started in the late 17th century when John Estell purchased thousands of acres along the Great Egg Harbor River, which later became home to a glassworks, gristmill, and sawmill. A furnace was established nearby. When these industries failed, the Estell family began selling off tracts of land. In 1910, the Bethlehem Loading Company saw this area as an ideal place to locate an ordnance proving ground, given that no towns were located within the 18,000-acre site. Five years later, the company began buying individual tracts of land that the Estells had sold off. With the advent of World War I, plans were changed to build a munitions plant instead. Ruins (left) are all that remain of the administration building vault that stood at the plant entrance. Below is an overview of the site. (Left, courtesy of photographer Andrew Gioulis; below, courtesy of the Hagley Museum and Library.)

This a view of the community in 1918. Built in about six months' time, it was to house 8,000 munitions workers and was designed to be self-contained—even having its own barbershop (below). Security, administration, and support buildings were constructed, along with shell-loading plants, housing for the workers, and a railroad that connected the community with bridges over the waterways. The Mays Landing plant was one of 14 shell-loading plants nationwide, 6 of which were in New Jersey. Bethlehem Loading Company owned three plants; this was its only site in New Jersey. (Both, courtesy of the Hagley Museum and Library.)

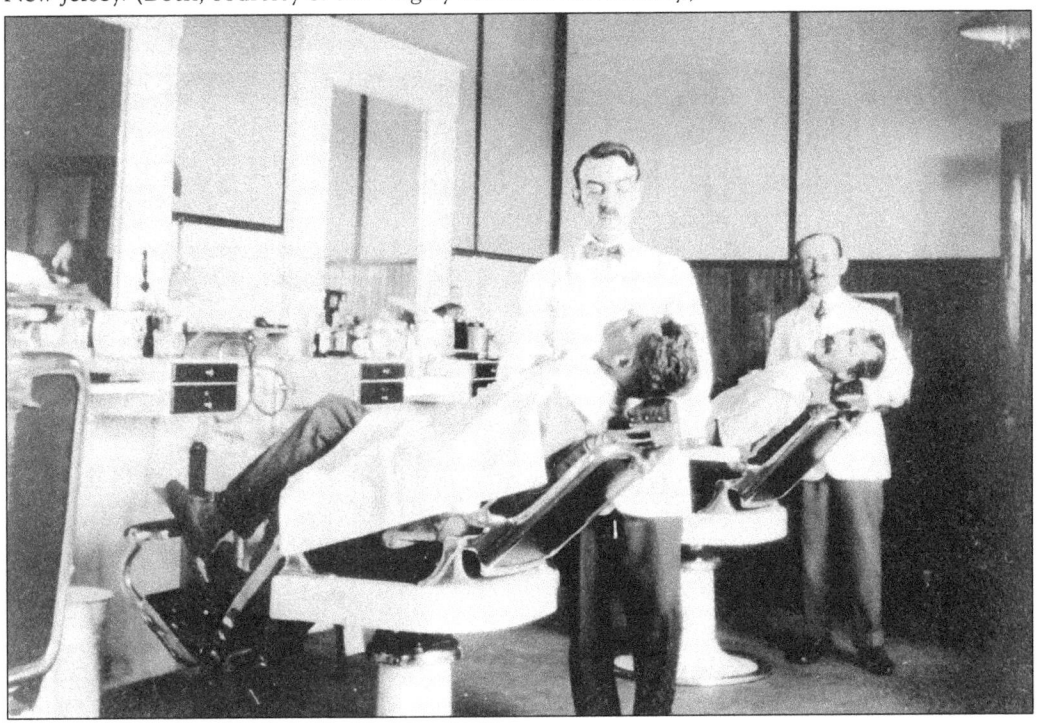

The site included 199 buildings, such as blacksmith, machine, and carpenter shops, one large cafeteria, two small cafeterias, a restaurant, and a stable for the police horses. It had its own water supply complex, sewage disposal plant, and a steam heat system. To service the shell assembly, pouring and receiving buildings, and shell storehouses, both broad and narrow gauge railroad systems were built. Footprints of these former railroad ties can still be seen in parts of the site today. Many of the buildings were made of reinforced concrete and steel. In fact, the water reservoir building, with its wall of eight-inch-thick concrete, still holds water today. (Both, courtesy of the Hagley Museum and Library.)

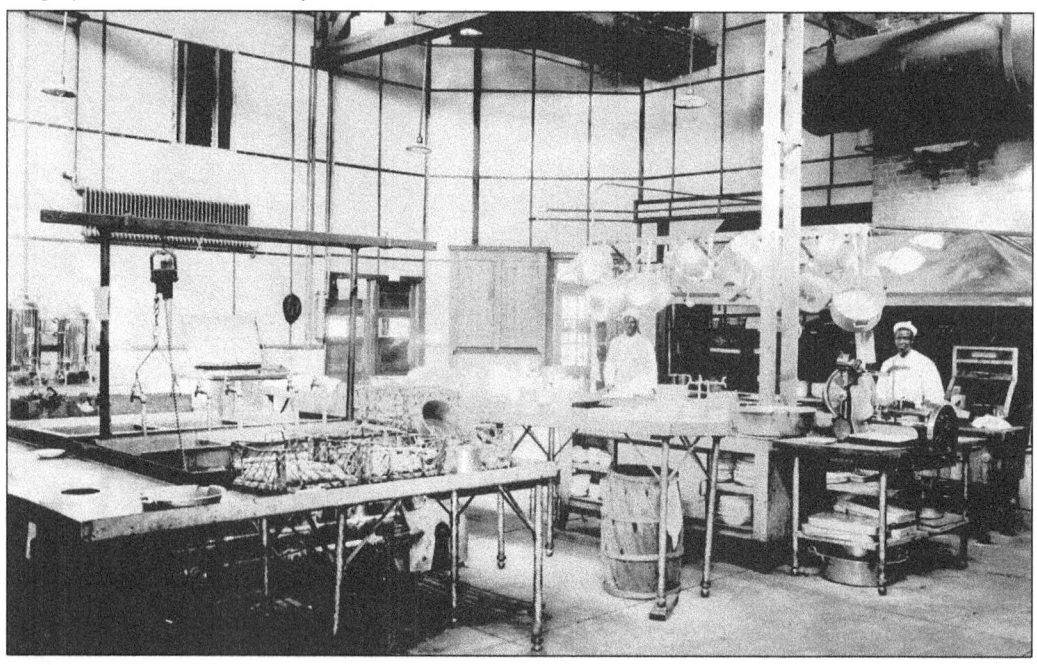

The plant and community were designed to provide for the loading and assembling of 75-millimeter, 155-millimeter, and 8-inch explosive shells. When the war ended in November 1918, the facility was without a mission but continued to load shells until February 1919 and then was a temporary munitions storage depot. In 1920, it was purchased by the federal government but was sold later that year to the Miles Company, which dismantled the buildings and sold the salvage. A 1,672-acre tract was used as a game preserve for several years and then sold in 1974 to the Atlantic County park system. Today, thanks to the work of historian Joan Berkey and with assistance from archaeologist Dick Regensburg, the site is now on both national and state historic registries. (Both, courtesy of the Hagley Museum and Library.)

The Tuckerton Wireless had been the world's eighth tallest structure when it was razed in December 1955; the historic landmark fell in less than six seconds. Built in Germany, the 800-ton, three-sided steel tower once rose 820 feet above the marshes on Mystic Island. It went into operation in 1914 and was used to make the first direct transatlantic radio transmission. Before then, messages had to be relayed ship-to-ship across the ocean. (Courtesy of the Tuckerton Historical Society.)

At the time, it was the second tallest radio tower in the world and the most powerful one in the United States. (Courtesy of the Tuckerton Historical Society.)

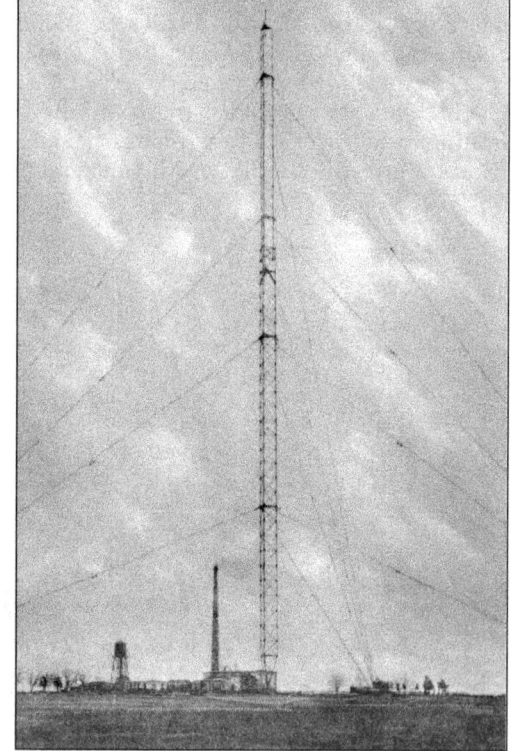

The Tuckerton Historical Society reported that the tower was controversial because it had been made in Germany and the war started shortly after its manufacture. Rumors abounded at the time that it was being used by spies to send messages. The U.S. Navy used the tower during World War II, and it was later sold to RCA. The base of the tower now rests in front of the Historical Society, where more information and photographs on the Wireless can be found. A 1951 scene of the interior of RCA Communications in Tuckerton (below) shows the alternators, induction motors, and control panels. The white line across the panels on the right is a high water mark. (Both, courtesy of the Tuckerton Historical Society.)

The Colliers Mills Wildlife Management Area is the northernmost part of the Pine Barrens. The name comes from the colliers who tended charcoal fires. Colliers Mills has an interesting past history of racetracks, a parachute tower, a thriving village, and cranberry bogs. Ephraim Emson, known as the Cranberry King, purchased over 15,000 acres of land throughout Ocean, Monmouth, and Burlington Counties. During the 1800s, Emson and his family lived on an estate in Colliers Mills where he raced horses and built a thriving village, parts of which are shown above. In the early 1900s, families would come to Colliers Mills Lake in the summer to swim and cool off (below) in the days before air conditioning. All of that changed when the state took ownership of the land and prohibited swimming. (Both, courtesy of the New Egypt Historical Society.)

On July 12, 1734, Indian John Pombelous sold his tract of land, which in part became Colliers Mills, to Edmund Beakes and his heirs for 30 shillings. Six others in his tribe and colonists Thomas Cobbs, James Frazee, and Anthony Woodward witnessed the deed shown here. It assigns the land, water, hunting rights, and all mines and quarries that exist on the land. (Courtesy of the Ocean County Cultural and Heritage Commission.)

In the days before the settlers came, the Lenni-Lenape hunted and fished in the Pine Barrens. Remnants of this old Indian dugout were found at Weymouth. Since then, the area has seen industries rise and fall and thriving villages become ghost towns. But thanks to the efforts of many, the Pine Barrens has been preserved, not only for hunting and fishing, but for the enjoyment of present and future generations. (Courtesy of the New Jersey Forest Service.)

Visit us at
arcadiapublishing.com

www.ingramcontent.com/pod-product-compliance
Lightning Source LLC
Chambersburg PA
CBHW081418160426

42813CB00087B/2189